# MIRACLES

## RELIVING THE MIRACLES OF JESUS

**PROJECT ENGINEER:** Lyman Coleman,
Serendipity House

**WRITERS FOR NOTES:** Richard Peace,
William Cutler

**WRITERS OF GROUP QUESTIONS:**
Lyman Coleman, Denny Rydberg

**COVER PHOTO:**
Robert Cushman Hayes

**TYPESETTING:** Sharon Penington,
Maurice Lydick, John Winson,
Douglas LaBudde

**PUBLISHER:** Serendipity House is a
resource community specializing in the
equipping of pastors and church leaders
for small group ministry in the local church
in the English speaking world. A list of
training events and resources can be
obtained by writing to the address below.

# SERENDIPITY GROUP BIBLE STUDY

Serendipity House / P.O.Box 1012 / Littleton, CO 80160

TOLL FREE 1-800-525-9563

Questions and Answers About

# Starting a Bible Study Group

**PURPOSE**

1.  *What is the purpose of a Bible study group?* Three things (and all three are important)

    a. Nurture—to be fed by God and grow in Christ, principally through Bible Study.

    b. Support—getting to know each other in a deeper way and caring for each other's needs.

    c. Mission—reaching out to non-churched people who are open to studying the Bible and reaching beyond your initial number until you can split into two groups . . . and keep multiplying.

**NON-CHURCHED**

2.  *How can people who don't go to church be interested in studying the Bible?* Pretty easy. In a recent survey, the Gallup Poll discovered that 74% of the people in America are looking for a spiritual faith.

**TURNED-OFF**

3.  *Then, why don't they go to church?* Because they have a problem with the institutional church.

**SEEKERS**

4.  *What are you suggesting?* That you start a Bible study group for these kinds of people.

    • People who are turned off by the church but are looking for a spiritual faith.

    • People who are struggling with personal problems and need a support group.

    • People who are crippled by a bad experience with the church and want to start over in their spiritual pilgrimage.

    • People who are down on themselves and need encouragement to see beyond their own shortcomings.

    • People who are looking for hope in the face of seemingly insurmountable difficulties.

    • People who flashed across your mind as you read over this list.

| | |
|---|---|
| **RECRUITING** | 5. *How do I get started?* Make a list of the "honest seekers you know" and keep this list on your refrigerator until you have asked everyone. |
| **FIRST MEETING** | 6. *What do we do at the first meeting?* Decide on your group covenant—a "contract" that spells out your expectations and rules (see the center section, page C5). |
| **DEVELOPING A CONTRACT** | 7. *How do we develop a contract?* Discuss these questions and ask someone to write down what you agree upon. (This "contract" will be used again at the close to evaluate your group). |

• What is the purpose of our group?

• What are the specific goals?

• How long are we going to meet? (We recommend 13 weeks. Then if you wish to continue, you can renew the contract).

• Where are we going to meet?

• What is going to be the starting and ending time at the sessions?

• What about babysitting/refreshments, etc.?

| | |
|---|---|
| **LIFECYCLE** | 8. *How long should a Bible study group last?* This should be taken in stages. (See flow chart below) |

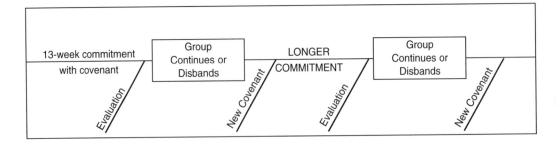

| | |
|---|---|
| **SHORT** | 9. *Why only a few weeks to start with?* Because people will give priority to something if they know it's not for long. And they can always renew and keep going if they wish. |
| **STUDY PLANS** | 10. *How do we go about the study of this book of the Bible?* This should be decided at the first meeting. Inside the front cover is a suggested schedule that you can follow. |
| **HOMEWORK** | 11. *Is there any homework?* No—unless you want to do some research about a particular concern. If you are studying one of the longer books of the Bible, where you do not have time to cover every passage, you may want to follow the "Reading" suggestions for this course of study. |
| **BIBLE IGNORANCE** | 12. *What if we have people in the group who know nothing about the Bible?* Great. This is what this group is all about. There are NOTES on the opposite page to refer to if you have any questions about a word, historical fact or significant person in the passage. |
| **NOTES** | 13. *Who wrote these Notes?* Richard Peace, a Professor at Gordon Conwell Seminary and a recognized Bible scholar. |
| **SERENDIPITY** | 14. *What is Serendipity?* A small research foundation that specializes in programs for support groups in a Christian context. |
| **DREAM** | 15. *What is your dream?* Christian support groups for hurting and struggling people inside and outside of the church—built around a study of Scripture and care for one another. For further information, we invite you to call:<br><br>TOLL FREE 1-800-525-9563, IN COLORADO 303-798-1313. |

# Introduction to
# MIRACLES

## What is a Miracle?

"I can't believe she said 'yes!' It's a miracle, but I'm going to marry her!"

"The 1980 USA Olympic Hockey Team was a miracle team, winning the gold medal when no one thought they would be able to do it."

"The fact that he could survive such a fall is a miracle."

"I never thought I could win the mega-bucks. It's a miracle!"

For a society that is by and large skeptical of the supernatural, we still attribute a great number of things to the realm of the miraculous! However, such diversity in the way this word is used forces us to ask the question "Just what do we mean when we call something a miracle?"

Behind each of the examples of the way the word "miracle" is used today lies the concept of an unexpected, tremendously beneficial event. God is not even necessarily involved; *any* stroke of unexpected good fortune is called a miracle. While the chances that any particular individual will win the mega-bucks are tiny, that *someone* will eventually win is simply a matter of the law of probability. None of the commentators who spoke of the 1980 USA Olympic hockey team's "miraculous" win of the gold medal would claim that God had somehow allowed USA shots to find their way into the goal while mysteriously causing the opponents' shots to miss their mark. The survival of a person after a great fall, while indeed rare and unexpected, can be experienced apart from the intervention of God. Reflecting this common use of the word "miracle," Roget's Thesaurus suggests the following words as possible synonyms: a marvel, a godsend, a serendipity, a bonanza, a stroke of luck, a phenomenon, a sensation, a spectacle, a boon, a windfall. Obviously, such an understanding of the miraculous does not capture the meaning of the miracles in the Bible, and specifically in the ministry of Jesus. In the Bible, miracles are not simply a matter of good fortune, but an example of the presence of God.

## Common Ideas About the Biblical Miracles

Everyone knows that the Bible tells of many miracles. The Old Testament records a host of miracle stories from the crossing of the Red Sea (Ex 14), to floating ax heads (2Ki 6), to the defeat of the Assyrian army when it was about to destroy Jerusalem (2Chr 32). The New Testament begins with the miracle story about the virgin birth of Jesus, and the whole of Jesus' ministry is accompanied by a variety of actions termed miracles. The apostles in Acts, likewise, are credited with the ability to perform healings and to raise the dead.

Popularly, it is thought that the Biblical miracles are events that happen contrary to nature. Indeed, there *are* stories of how God altered natural forces. The Red Sea was divided by a great wind. Severe plagues afflicted the Egyptians but spared the Israelites. Elijah was able to provide for the needs of a poor widow through the never-emptying flask of oil and always full jar of flour. Elisha made an ax head float. Jesus walked on water, silenced a storm by a single command, fed the five thousand with a few loaves of bread and a couple of fish, and turned water into wine at a wedding. Elijah, Elisha, Jesus, Peter, and Paul all raised at least one dead person to life. These accounts do require an over-ruling or a suspension of what we call natural laws. However, there are other types of miracle stories as well which do not necessarily involve actions contrary to nature.

For instance, there are many cases of healing. In these stories sick people recover immediately. While some of the healings were of people who otherwise would have died of their illness, other healings simply speeded up the normal recovery process. Jesus healed many blind or lame people, but recovery from blindness and paralysis is attested in modern times as well in cases of psychosomatic reactions to trauma.

There are also miracles of decisive victory over forces of entrenched evil. These are particularly true of Jesus' exorcism of demons. Other people in Jesus' day (and before and since) have demonstrated such abilities as well.

Finally, there are instances of the foreknowledge of events. The fact that Peter caught a fish with a coin in its mouth is not all that remarkable in itself. What is remarkable is that Jesus told him it would happen (Mt 17:27)! However, many people would argue that instances of clairvoyance are not unique to Jesus.

From this survey, we can see that the miracles in the Bible come in a variety of forms. They do not necessarily involve exceptions to what we call the natural order. As we shall see, their distinctiveness lies elsewhere.

Another common opinion about the miracles of the Bible is that they are simply meant to prove that the one who performs them is a messenger from God. While this was true in some cases (as when Moses was allowed to perform certain miraculous acts to prove to the Israelites that he had indeed been sent by God), such a view does not do justice to the miracles of Jesus. It is true that the miracles pointed to the uniqueness of Jesus: "The miracle-worker Jesus is unlike anything in ordinary experience. He arouses amazement and wonder. Where he appears, a gap is made in the fabric of ordinary, everyday experience: 'We never saw anything like this' (Mark 2:12)."[1] His actions led people to ponder his identity and the significance of his actions.

However, the miracles revealed God's presence and power only to those who saw with the eyes of faith. Jesus' miracles were interpreted in widely different ways. Although many people saw them as evidence of the presence of God, others viewed them as acts of Satan intended to deceive people. (Mt 12:22f). As such, they do not *prove* Jesus' divine authority, but are pointers to it to those whose hearts and minds are open to him.

A major difficulty with the idea that miracles were primarily proofs of Jesus' authority is that Jesus repudiated this view several times! He refused to follow Satan's suggestion to stage a miraculous deliverance to prove that he was the Son of God (Mt 4:6–7). He rejected the Pharisees' request for a sign to authenticate his authority (Mk 8:11–12). Indeed, it was the miracles themselves that often produced intense conflict with established religious authorities. The religious establishment lived comfortably with healing cults (such as is referred to in John 5:1ff) and other people who possessed abilities to heal, but Jesus' miracles were seen as being in opposition to sacred traditions and laws. He healed on the Sabbath and made claims to divine prerogatives (Mk 3:1–5; 2:1–12). These actions created a crisis by forcing people to choose between him and the established traditions. It is especially interesting to note that particularly in Mark's account, many of the miracles were performed in secret with express orders for the people involved *not* to tell anyone what happened lest Jesus be misunderstood. The miracles were not in themselves irresistible proofs of Jesus' deity.

The biggest problem with this view, however, is that it makes miracles essentially unnecessary and without inherent meaning. Instead, they become only wonders done to amaze the crowds and get them to listen to Jesus.

**The Miracles As Message**

It is far more in accord with the nature of Jesus' miracles to see them as an essential part of his message. The message would not be the same without the miracles. They are the physical demonstrations of the news he announced regarding the inbreaking of the kingdom of God. Without the miracles, Jesus would simply have been another prophet looking ahead to the coming of the kingdom. The healing of the blind, the lame, the leprous, and the deaf as well as the raising of the dead and the proclamation of the good news of God's kingdom (Mt 11:4–5), all together point to the truth that in Jesus the kingdom of God has indeed begun to break in upon the world.

The Gospel of John especially illustrates the importance of the miracles as being part and parcel of Jesus' message. This Gospel is built around seven miracle stories which it calls "signs." That very term reveals an important insight about the way John viewed the miracles. They are not simply stories of Jesus' amazing power meant to get people's attention, nor are they simply acts of compassion for those who benefit by them. Rather, they reveal the nature of his kingdom. Colin Brown makes an important observation in this regard when he writes: "(The miracles) are signs of God's kingly rule, the dawn of which Jesus announced in his proclamation ... the miracles are a foreshadowing and a promise of the coming universal redemption ... Thus, the casting out of demons signals God's invasion into the realm of Satan and its final annihilation; the raising of the dead announces that death will be forever done away with; the healing of the sick bears witness to the cessation of all suffering; the miraculous provisions of food are foretokens of the end of all physical need; the stilling of the storm points forward to the complete victory over the powers of chaos which threaten the earth."[2]

In the same vein, Karl Barth notes, "What took place (in the miracles) were promises and ... anticipations of a ... kind of life in which there will be no more sorrow, tears, and crying, and where death as the last enemy will be no more."[3]

Seen in this way, the miracle stories of Jesus become important signs of what God's kingdom (as well as the King) is all about. They demonstrate God's opposition to disease, chaos, suffering, and death. In Christ, God has come to free people from the power of these forces. The miracles are therefore glimpses of what the Kingdom of God truly means. They reflect the values and truths for which God's people are to work and pray. They accent Jesus' authority over all forces that oppress humanity. Demons, sickness, nature, and death itself are subject to Jesus. His miracles imply an authority to which people must become subject and illustrate the presence of a kingdom in which people are invited to participate.

### The Problem of Miracles Today

Many people struggle with the whole notion of miracles. While they used to be seen as proof of the Christian claims to truth, now many Christians consider the miracle stories as somewhat embarrassing relics that seem out of place with the modern world. They are something like the relatives you hope your friends never meet: you can't deny they are part of your history, but you aren't quite sure how to explain their presence!

Such a concern stems from a world view that gained prominence during the Enlightenment. Simply put, it has no place for the miraculous because it has no place for a God who acts in history. While the Biblical authors believed in God's sovereignty over all events, people today are conditioned to think in terms of natural laws, cause and effect, and physical properties. If any credence at all is given to the supernatural, it is assumed that there is a clear division between matters of nature and matters of the spirit. While such a view might acknowledge that the spiritual dimension is important for a person's inner life, it would deny there is any relationship between the spiritual realm and the "reality" of the natural world.

The world view of the Biblical authors, however, was not divided into separate, watertight "sacred" and "secular" compartments. "Natural law" was simply not thought of at this time. Instead, they viewed all of life as under God's control all of the time. The coming of the spring rain was not seen as the result of a complex weather pattern but as the gift of God to replenish the earth. Thus, the miraculous was not seen as a breaking of some independent law of nature or as an absolutely unexplainable event apart from God's intervention, but as a demonstration of the special presence of God. The spiritual realm was seen to have great impact upon the physical.

In contrast, modern technological society views historical and physical events as simply the product of natural forces. It assumes the world is a closed system of cause and effect which can be studied and understood. By its very definition, such an approach rules out the possibility of supernatural intervention. However, this view does not *disprove* the Biblical miracles; it simply *assumes* such things could not happen and seeks alternative explanations.

The real issue is a matter of faith. Either we believe, like the Biblical writers, that there is a God who is free to intervene in his creation, or we believe that the world is a closed system of cause and effect through natural forces. Both positions begin with an assumption and interpret events in the light of that assumption. It is not as though those who believe in the latter view have more information or insight than those who believe the former, nor does it imply that those who believe in the reality of miracles are somehow ignorant of the scientific discoveries of the past 400 years. Those who believe in miracles (whose number includes many scientists) simply see no compelling reason to rule out the possibility of God's intervention in what is called the "natural" world. They recognize that disbelief in the possibility of miracles is not a scientific position, but a philosophical commitment made for other reasons.

### Can Miracles Happen Today?

Do miracles still happen?

In the Bible, miracles cluster around those times when God moves history toward its final goal in an especially powerful, significant way. "God does not shake miracles into Nature at random as if from a pepper-caster. They come on great occasions... of that spiritual history which cannot be fully known by men (*sic*) ..."[4] There are the dramatic stories of God's power associated with the Exodus and the conquest of the Promised Land, yet after that Israel went for centuries with only rare demonstrations of power. Elijah and Elisha, the first of the great prophets, performed miracles but Isaiah, Jeremiah, and Ezekiel did not. By far, most of Israel's history was not marked by miracles. Spirituality was not a matter of having power to perform wondrous acts but a matter of acting justly, loving mercy, and walking humbly with God (Mi 6:8).

The New Testament never calls upon Christians to "expect a miracle" to relieve them of the common pains of life or to convince doubters of the Gospel. Miracles, like the water becoming wine, the feeding of the five thousand, and the raising of Lazarus were special signs highlighting Jesus' identity and depicting the life he will give to all when the kingdom is fully revealed. The church today probably should not expect miracles such as these. These were meant to anticipate what the final reality of God's people will be like, not a taste of what day-to-day life in Christ will bring.

But what about the boy whose leg was healed after prayer or the cancer-ridden patient who was suddenly found to have no traces of disease? How does one account for the softening of a hard-hearted person such that they believe the Gospel? What about the strange circumstances that "just happened" so that a person was protected from some harm that otherwise would have occurred? Such stories are frequent enough that many Christians believe that God still intervenes in miraculous ways, especially in the areas of healings, exorcisms, and conversions.

The Scripture certainly encourages people to pray with the expectation that prayer makes a difference. The deist conception of the world as a clock created by a cosmic watchmaker that is then left to run on its own does not reflect a Biblical understanding neither of God nor the world. The Scripture describes God as the Living God precisely because the writers believe that God acts in history. Thus, it is not for us to rule out the possibility of God's intervention at any time.

However, those who do not experience such dramatic acts must never feel they are second-class citizens of the kingdom. Most Christians throughout history have not seen a miracle. Fervent prayers for healing or deliverance from harm often go unanswered. If we believe God is free to intervene at any point for his purposes, we must also believe he is free from being controlled by human interests or desires. Instead, we must embrace the truth that God is free to act at any time, in any place, in any way, for his purposes and glory.

However, this should not be an excuse for a lazy faith that reflects more of the modern notion that God is separate and rather uninvolved in his creation. "The malady of our time lies in its contracted thoughts of God. We think too narrowly and meanly of His Power, His Love, and His Freedom to help … That is what the miracles of Jesus and His teachings about faith mean … God is more near, more real and mighty, more full of love, and more ready to help every one of us than any one of us realizes, that is (the miracles) undying message." [5]

## Studying the Miracles of Jesus

We are going to look at the miracles of Jesus by first examining one of the greatest of all miracles, the Incarnation: God becomes man (Unit 1). Then we will look at Jesus' power over illness (Units 2–4), over demons (Units 5–6) and over nature (Units 7–10). Finally, we will look at Jesus' power over death itself (Units 11–13). In looking at these various types of miracles we gain new and valuable insight into who Jesus is and into the nature of his kingdom. We grow in our awareness of this amazing person, and we are challenged anew to be a part of his work in the world.

[1] Gerd Thiessen, *The Miracle Stories of the Early Christian Tradition*, T. and T. Clark, 1983, p. 301.
[2] Colin Brown (ed.), *Dictionary of New Testament Theology*, Vol. 11, *Miracle*.
[3] Karl Barth, *Evangelical Theology: An Introduction*, p. 68–69.
[4] C.S. Lewis, *Miracles*, p.174.
[5] D.S. Cairns, *The Faith That Rebels*, Richard Smith Inc., 1930. pp. 246–247.

# UNIT 1—The Birth of Jesus / Luke 1:26–38; 2:1–7

## Scripture

The Birth of Jesus Foretold

*26In the sixth month, God sent the angel Gabriel to Nazareth, a town in Galilee, 27to a virgin pledged to be married to a man named Joseph, a descendant of David. The virgin's name was Mary. 28The angel went to her and said, "Greetings, you who are highly favored! The Lord is with you."*

*29Mary was greatly troubled at his words and wondered what kind of greeting this might be. 30But the angel said to her, "Do not be afraid, Mary, you have found favor with God. 31You will be with child and give birth to a son, and you are to give him the name Jesus. 32He will be great and will be called[a] the Son of the Most High. The Lord God will give him the throne of his father David, 33and he will reign over the house of Jacob forever; his kingdom will never end."*

*34"How will this be," Mary asked the angel, "since I am a virgin?"*

*35The angel answered, "The Holy Spirit will come upon you, and the power of the Most High will overshadow you.[a] So the holy one to be born will be called the Son of God. 36Even Elizabeth your relative is going to have a child in her old age, and she who was said to be barren is in her sixth month. 37For nothing is impossible with God."*

*38"I am the Lord's servant," Mary answered. "May it be to me as you have said." Then the angel left her.*

The Birth of Jesus

*2In those days Caesar Augustus issued a decree that a census should be taken of the entire Roman world. 2(This was the first census that took place while Quirinius was governor of Syria.) 3And everyone went to his own town to register.*

*4So Joseph also went up from the town of Nazareth in Galilee to Judea, to Bethlehem the town of David, because he*

*was pledged to be married to him and was expecting a child. 6While they were there, the time came for the baby to be born, 7and she gave birth to her firstborn, a son. She wrapped him in cloths and placed him in a manger, because there was no room for them in the inn.*

---

[a]35 or [So the child *to be born* will be called holy,]

*belonged to the house and line of David. 5He went there to register with Mary, who*

10

# Group Questions

Every group meeting has three parts: **(1) To Begin** (15 minutes) to break the ice; **(2) Read Scripture and Discuss** (30 Minutes); and **(3) To Close and Pray** (15-30 Minutes). Try to keep on schedule. The most important time is the prayer time.

**TO BEGIN / 15 Minutes** (Choose 1 or 2)

❏ Where were you born? In the hospital or at home?
❏ How did you get your name? Who are you named after?
❏ If God told you that you were going to be a parent nine months from now, how would you feel?

**READ SCRIPTURE AND DISCUSS / 30 Minutes**

❏ How would you compare the way Luke (a physician) wrote up this account of the birth of Christ ... to the way doctors write up births today?
❏ Why would Luke, the author, be so careful to document the historical facts surrounding Jesus' birth?
❏ What do you learn about Jesus Christ in the angel's announcement? Do you think Mary understood what she was getting into?
❏ Do you think the humble beginnings of Mary and Joseph's marriage and Jesus' birth were coincidental, or part of the plan and purpose of God?
❏ Mothers: How did you break the news to your husband that you were going to have a baby?
❏ Fathers: What was your first thought when you heard that you were going to be a father?
❏ When did you come to understand the meaning of the birth of Christ? Who was the "angel" that explained the truth about Jesus to you?
❏ How would you describe your relationship with Jesus Christ now?

**TO CLOSE AND PRAY / 15–30 Minutes**

❏ Why did you join this Bible study group? What would you like to get out of this group?
❏ Who else do you think would benefit by being in this group?
❏ How can this group help you in prayer this week?

# Notes

**Summary.** To discuss the miracles of Jesus requires that we begin with what C. S. Lewis calls "the Grand Miracle": the incarnation. God becomes man. "Every other miracle prepares for this, or exhibits this, or results from this." Jesus came down from heaven and became a man—a man like every other man. He walked. He talked. He ate. He was of a particular height and weight. He had hair and eyes of a particular color. But he was also God.

That God should and could enter time and space as a human baby is breathtaking in its audacity. In the first century Greco-Roman world gods did not behave like this. To be sure gods sometimes had human forms. Even the Roman emperors were considered to be gods. But these Roman and Greek gods were at the top of the social heap, not at the bottom. They had all power, not no power. In the Jewish world it was also a question of power. When the Messiah came (and he was considered a representative of God, not the One God whose name was too sacred to be uttered), he would be invincible: a mighty warrior who would slay the enemies of Israel and set up a world wide throne in Jerusalem. That the mighty creator God who made heaven and earth would come as a little baby crying in a stable was simply inconceivable. Yet, this is just what happened.

The story of the incarnation of Jesus is found at various places in the NT (Mt 1:18–2:23; John 1:1–18), and alluded to in other places (Mark 1:11; 9:7; Gal 4:4–5; Phil 2:6–8; and Col 1:15–20). We are going to look at two sections of Luke's account. Prior to the first passage the birth of John the Baptist has been foretold (Luke 1:5–25). Then the birth of Jesus is foretold (the first passage we will study). Next, Mary visits Elizabeth and they share their stories (Luke 1:39–45). Mary's great song of rejoicing follows next in the account (Lk 1:46–56). Then come the story of the birth of John the Baptist (Luke 1:57–66), Zechariah's song (Luke 1:67–80) and, finally, the birth of Jesus (the second passage we will study).

**1:26 *In the sixth month.*** This is the sixth month of Elizabeth's pregnancy.

***Nazareth ... a town in Galilee.*** Nazareth was an insignificant little village in the province of Galilee (John 1:46).

**1:27 *a virgin pledged to be married.*** Betrothal, usually lasting for about a year, could occur as young as 12 years of age. This was a far more binding arrangement than engagements today. Although sexual relations were not permitted, the woman had the legal status of a wife and the relationship could only be broken by divorce. The virgin birth of Jesus traces its roots to the prophecy of the child spoken of in Isaiah 7:14: "The Lord himself will give you a sign: The virgin will be with child and will give birth to a son, and will call him Immanuel."

**Joseph, a descendant of David.** The Messiah was to come through the line of David, the most famous king of Israel's history (2Sa 7:16; Ps 132:11).

**1:28 you who are highly favored.** The angel is not commending her virtue, but recognizing the reality of God's grace to her.

**The Lord is with you.** This is often used as a statement of God's special intention to equip a person for his service (see Jos 1:5; Jdg 6:12; Mt 28:20).

**1:31** This sentence, clearly quoting Isaiah 7:14, firmly links Mary's experience with Isaiah's prophecy. The child foretold in Isaiah 7:14 was to be named Immanuel, which means "God with us." Jesus was a common Jewish name meaning "God saves."

**1:32 He will be great ... the Son of the Most High.** Jesus, like John the Baptist (Lk 1:15), will be considered "great", but the greatness of these two men will be of differing orders. John is great "in the eyes of the Lord" (Lk 1:5) as "a prophet of the Most High (Lk 1:76), but Jesus' greatness consists in his being the Son of the Most High. While verse 35 indicates that Jesus' "sonship" does reflect the mystery of the shared nature of the Father and Son, this particular phrase is a title (applied to Israel's kings in the OT) reflecting the God-given authority to rule over God's people (2Sa 7:14; Ps 82:6).

**the throne of his father David.** As the Messianic prophecy of Isaiah 9:1–7 indicates, the Son of God will rule over Israel.

**1:34 How will this be? ...** Zechariah asked this question of the angel when informed that he and his wife Elizabeth would have a child (Lk 1:18). He asked out of doubt that such a thing could happen. Mary, however, is expressing wonder, no doubt.

**1:35 The Holy Spirit ... the power of the Most high.** Parallelism was a common device of Hebrew

poetry. In this form, the phrases are meant to simply echo one another; they do not imply two different things.

**will overshadow you.** This term is used to describe God's presence in the temple (Ex 40:35). While it implies God's presence with Mary, there is no hint as to the means of conception.

**the holy one to be born will be called the Son of God.** Jews considered every first-born child as "holy" to the Lord in the sense of being set apart for him (Ex 13:12), but this carries the idea of holiness in the sense of being "God-like." While the sonship of verse 32 indicated Jesus' title and role, this reference to Sonship indicates his nature and being as God incarnate.

**1:37 Nothing is impossible with God.** The ultimate ground for Mary's faith rests on this fact. In similar circumstances, when Sarah laughed at the idea that a woman her age could have a child, God said "Is anything too hard for the Lord?" (Ge 18:14). It was this conviction that gave Biblical figures courage and faith in the hardest of times (Jer 32:27; Mk 10:27).

**1:38 I am the Lord's servant.** The rejection, embarrassment, and fear that Mary would face as a result of this pregnancy is accepted with this confession of her complete submission to God. "Mary had learned to forget the world's commonest prayer —'Thy will be changed' - and to pray the world's greatest prayer - 'Thy will be done' "(Barclay).

**2:1 Caesar Augustus.** He ruled the Roman Empire from 30 B.C. to 14 A.D.

**census.** From about 30 B.C. onward, the Ceasars ordered people in the various Roman provinces to report every 14 years for a census for purposes of taxation. Resistance from the population and from local rulers sometimes meant census taking required several years to complete. While there is firm evidence of a census after King Herod's death in 6 A.D., there is no external source that allows us to know whether the census mentioned here was a separate, earlier one or the beginning stages of the census completed at that date.

**1:3–4 everyone went to his own town.** Since Joseph and Mary lived in Galilee, they must have owned some property in Bethlehem. Roman custom required people who owned property in another location from where they lived to register there as well. Bethlehem, a three to four day journey from Galilee, was the village where King David, through whose line the Messiah was to come, had lived.

**1:5 *to register with Mary.*** In some provinces, the Romans charged a poll tax on women 12 years of age or older.

***pledged to be married to him and was expecting a child.*** Their betrothal had not yet been consummated by intercourse (see Mt 1:24–25).

**1:6–7** While in Bethlehem, the time for birth arrived. Thus a political decision by the Roman emperor led to the fulfillment of the prophecy in Micah 5:2: "But you, Bethlehem Ephrathah, though you are small among the clans of Judah, out of you will come for me one who will be ruler over Israel, whose origins are from of old, from ancient times."

**1:7 *firstborn.*** The firstborn of every Jewish family was dedicated to God in a special way (Ex 13:12). This firstborn son would be dedicated in a way unlike any other child.

***manger.*** A feeding trough for animals.

***the inn.*** This word can mean either a building used for the accommodation of travelers or a spare room in a private home. Whichever the case, there was no space available for the couple. Instead, they had to stay with the animals. A tradition dating back to the second century maintains that they stayed in a cave which was used as a barn.

# Down Through Time and Space
—by C. S. Lewis

In the Christian story God descends to re-ascend. He comes down; down from the heights of absolute being into time and space, down into humanity; down further still, if embryologists are right, to recapitulate in the womb ancient and pre-human phases of life; down to the very roots and seabed of the Nature He has created. But He goes down to come up again and bring the whole ruined world up with Him. One has the picture of a strong man stooping lower and lower to get himself underneath some great complicated burden. He must stoop in order to lift, he must almost disappear under the load before he incredibly straightens his back and marches off with the whole mass swaying on his shoulders. Or one may think of a diver, first reducing himself to nakedness, then glancing in mid-air, then gone with a splash, vanished, rushing down through green and warm water into black and cold water, down through increasing pressure into the death-like region of ooze and slime and old decay; then up again, back to colour and light, his lungs almost bursting, till suddenly he breaks surface again, holding in his hand the dripping, precious thing that he went down to recover. He and it are both colored now that they have come up into the light: down below, where it lay colorless in the dark, he lost his colour too. (*Miracles*, London: Collins [Fontana Books] 1947, chapter 14, pp. 115–116.)

# UNIT 2—Jesus Heals a Paralytic / Mark 2:1–12

## Scripture

Jesus Heals a Paralytic

**2**¹*A few days later, when Jesus again entered Capernaum, the people heard that he had come home. ²So many gathered that there was no room left, not even outside the door, and he preached the word to them. ³Some men came, bringing to him a paralytic, carried by four of them. ⁴Since they could not get him to Jesus because of the crowd, they made an opening in the roof above Jesus and, after digging through it, lowered the mat the paralyzed man was lying on. ⁵When Jesus saw their faith, he said to the paralytic, "Son, your sins are forgiven."*

*⁶Now some teachers of the law were sitting there, thinking to themselves, ⁷"Why does this fellow talk like that? He's blaspheming! Who can forgive sins but God alone?"*

*⁸Immediately Jesus knew in his spirit that this was what they were thinking in their hearts, and he said to them, "Why are you thinking these things? ⁹Which is easier: to say to the paralytic, 'Your sins are forgiven,' or to say, 'Get up, take your mat and walk'? ¹⁰But that you may know that the Son of Man has authority on earth to forgive sins ... " He said to the paralytic, ¹¹"I tell you, get up, take your mat and go home." ¹²He got up, took his mat and walked out in full view of them all. This amazed everyone and they praised God, saying, "We have never seen anything like this!"*

# Group Questions

Every group meeting has three parts: **(1) To Begin** (15 minutes) to break the ice; **(2) Read Scripture and Discuss** (30 Minutes); and **(3) To Close and Pray** (15–30 Minutes). Try to keep on schedule. The most important time is the prayer time.

## TO BEGIN / 15 Minutes (Choose 1 or 2)

- ❏ When you were little, who did you go to with a hurt finger?
- ❏ When is the last time you had to rush to the emergency ward at the hospital?
- ❏ If you knew someone could help a hurting friend, how far would you go to get your friend to this person?

## READ SCRIPTURE AND DISCUSS / 30 Minutes

- ❏ If something like this happened on Sunday in your church, what would the people say: "Let's not get carried away?" "Who is going to pay for the roof?" "We're for anything that is going to help someone?"
- ❏ What impresses you about the four friends in this story?
- ❏ What do you think was going on in the minds of the principal characters in this story? The owner of the house? The teachers of the Law? The paralytic himself?
- ❏ Why are the teachers of the law so upset? (See Note on next page.)
- ❏ What exactly is the miracle here: A physical healing? A crippling emotional healing? A spiritual healing?
- ❏ Why didn't Jesus just heal the man like everyone expected?
- ❏ What is the closest you have come to experiencing this kind of healing in your life?
- ❏ What is the closest you have been to being in a support group that cared for you when you were hurting?

## TO CLOSE AND PRAY / 15–30 Minutes

- ❏ Do you feel comfortable sharing the area in your own life where you need healing with this group?
- ❏ Do you have the faith that the four friends had in the healing power of Jesus Christ?
- ❏ How could this group help you in prayer this week?

# Notes

**Summary.** We begin our examination of the miracles of Jesus by looking at his power over illness. It was his ability to heal people that drew large crowds to him (see Mark 3:7–10). This is not at all surprising in a day and age in which there were no hospitals, no reliable doctors (see Mark 5:25–26), no antibiotics, and only rudimentary procedures and drugs. The life span was short. Illness was the enemy. Parents lived in dread of childhood diseases that wiped out their families. Thus when Jesus appeared and actually cured a wide range of diseases, the people were overjoyed. Paralysis was a common ailment in the middle east. Sometimes the inability to use a limb was congenital. However, people were mostly crippled as the result of an accident or because of a disease such as polio. In this story, the illness was not psychosomatic (see Note on 2:3). Clearly, here Jesus heals organic damage to the man's spine. Such a healing is a miracle in the true sense, an act that goes well beyond the skill of medicine or psychology.

While this story deals with healing and with faith, this is not its central point. The point of the story is the revelation by Jesus of who he is: the Son of Man who, like God, has the power to forgive sin.

**2:1 *A few days later.*** Each of the five incidents in Mark 2:1–3:6 is introduced by this sort of indefinite time measure (Mark 2:13,18,23; 3:1) indicating that these incidents probably did not happen in sequence, one right after the other. Mark's interest was not chronology. Instead, by grouping stories together around various themes he hopes to reveal to his readers who Jesus is.

***home.*** Capernaum served as Jesus' base for his travels in Galilee. Quite possibly this was the home of Peter and Andrew (Mark 1:29,32–33).

**2:3 *some men.*** Apparently the paralytic had not been healed on Jesus' previous visit. His friends do not want to let this new opportunity pass.

***a paralytic.*** Luke, the doctor, uses (in Greek) a technically more exact phrase to describe this man's illness (Luke 5:18). From that we understand that he was, apparently, a paraplegic with spinal damage.

***carried by four of them.*** They probably each took hold of one corner of his mat.

# Notes (Continued)

**2:2 *So many gathered.*** On Jesus' previous visit to Capernaum (Mark 1:16–34) he healed many people and cast out demons from others. Then he left in order to preach in other villages (Mark 1:35–39). No wonder there was great interest in him when he returned. News of his return would have spread quickly in a village, so much so that the home he went to (which was quite small) was quickly filled. People were probably standing in the open-air courtyard, listening from windows, etc.

**he preached the word to them.** Although Mark does not record much of Jesus' preaching, he continually points out that announcing the news of the kingdom of God was Jesus' primary agenda (Mark 1:14–15,38; 2:13; 3:14; 4:1; 6:2,12,34). The miracles he performed were intended as illustrations and examples of what life in the kingdom which he proclaimed would be like. However, the crowds typically were far more attracted to the fact of the miracles than to their meaning!

**2:4 *an opening in the roof.*** The roof of a typical Palestinian house was flat (it was often used for sleeping) and was reached by an outside ladder or stairway. It was constructed of earth and brushwood that was packed between wooden beams set about three feet apart. This type of roof was easily opened up (and could easily be repaired).

**mat.** The bed of a poor person.

**2:5 *saw their faith.*** Jesus' act of forgiveness and healing is connected to faith. In this case it is the faith of the paralytic's friends. Their faith was shown in the fact that they went to collect the paralytic and that they overcame in a very clever, determined way the obstacle which prevented them from bringing their friend to Jesus. Both these acts testify to their deep conviction that Jesus could and would heal the man. It is interesting that it is the faith of the friends that is pointed out. Nothing is said about the faith of the paralytic (at this point). In the next unit it is the faith of the woman with chronic bleeding that is mentioned. Sometimes faith is not mentioned at all when it comes to healing (e.g., 1:32–33). The lack of faith is said to make healing impossible. For example, when Jesus returns to his hometown of Nazareth he heals few (Mark 6:1–6). Jesus comments on the lack of faith of the people of Nazareth (Mark 6:6). Apparently they did not believe Jesus could heal (because of their prejudice against him which is described in the

story) so they did not bother to bring the ill to him. The faith that is demonstrated here is defined as "confident, believing trust" (Mann). It is not just the belief that something is possible. It is an "energetic grasping of the help and power of God" (Fuller).

**your sins are forgiven.** This was not what the crowd expected Jesus to say. They anticipated that he would say "You are healed." Jesus says what he does so as to declare to the religious leaders who he is claiming to be.

**2:6 *teachers of the law.*** These are, literally, the "scribes," men who acted as religious lawyers, interpreting Jewish law. Originally, it was their job to make copies of the OT. Because of their familiarity with Scripture, people consulted them about points of law and hence their role evolved into that of teacher and protector of the law. Luke's account of this story (Luke 5:17ff) states that the scribes had come from "every village of Galilee and from Judea and Jerusalem" indicating that this was an official delegation sent to investigate the orthodoxy of this unknown, enormously popular teacher.

**2:7 *this fellow.*** This is a term of contempt.

**blaspheming.** Blasphemy is the act of expressing contempt for God or usurping the rights of God. Under Jewish law its penalty is death (Lev 24:16). The teachers of the law believed that illness was the direct result of sin (e.g. Jn 9:2), so that the sick could not recover until their sin had been forgiven by God. They also knew that God alone could offer forgiveness. Hence they are distressed that Jesus has said to the paralytic "your sins are forgiven." This was to claim in quite explicit terms that he was divine and this was the vilest blasphemy.

**Who can forgive sins but God alone?** This is an accurate understanding of the OT scripture. Since sin, despite whatever social consequences it may entail, is primarily an offense against God and his law, only God is in the position to offer forgiveness.

**2:8** Jesus knows what they are thinking—whether by their body language, by his knowledge of how they would react, or by his divine insight.

**2:9 *which is easier.*** Jesus responds to their question (v. 7) in typical rabbinic fashion: he asks them a question. The answer to his question is obvious. It is

16

far easier to say "Your sins are forgiven" than it is to heal the man right then and there. There is no way to verify whether sins have been forgiven but it is obvious whether a lame man walks or not.

**2:10 *but that you may know ... to forgive sins.*** If Jesus is able to heal the paralytic the scribes would have to admit that he had, indeed, forgiven the man's sins since their own theology linked forgiveness and healing. The visible healing would verify the invisible forgiveness. If they were consistent, the teachers of the law would now have to admit that Jesus was God (or at least a representative of God) because it is they who said "Who can forgive sins but God alone?" (v. 7).

***the Son of Man.*** This is the first use of this title in the Gospel of Mark to describe Jesus. This was a nondescript title, meaning "Sir" or "a human being." In the story probably no one paid much attention to it. However, Son of Man is a title that is tinged with Messianic content. Its roots go back to Daniel 7:13f in which the prophet sees a vision of one "like a son of man" receiving authority to rule over God's kingdom. It seems that Jesus chose such a neutral title for himself (it is his favorite self-designation) so that he could fill it with distinct content. In unit 4 of Mark's Gospel (8:31–10:52) he does define what it means: "The Son of Man ... [came] to give his life as a ransom for many" (Mk 10:45).

***authority on earth.*** The words "on earth" are better understood as referring to the place where sins are committed, i.e. "has authority to forgive sins on earth."

***to forgive sins.*** Mark typically uses short, one line sentences to communicate the essence of Jesus' ministry (e.g. 1:15, 38; 2:17). This sentence communicates the central thrust of Jesus' mission toward which this miracle was intended to point: Jesus has the power to forgive sin. This is the essential message of this story, and the message of the Gospel.

**2:11 *I tell you.*** This focuses attention on the authority of Jesus himself. He does not invoke any other name but his own. It is through his divine power that the man is healed (and, by extension, forgiven of sin).

***He got up, took his mat and walked out.*** Up to this point the focus has been on the faith of the friends. Now the attention is turned to the paralytic. Jesus has just asked him to act in faith (v. 11). Now the paralytic has to trust that he has, indeed, been healed and actually struggle to get up and walk, something he had not been able to do previously.

**2:12 *This amazed everyone.*** Mark's miracle stories often end with an observation of the amazement on the part of those who witnessed the event. The "everyone" would not seem to include the teachers of the Law who from this time on became more and more resistant to Jesus.

# UNIT 3—A Sick Woman Touches Jesus / Mark 5:24–34

## Scripture

A Sick Woman Touches Jesus

[24]*So Jesus went with him. A large crowd followed and pressed around him.* [25]*And a woman was there who had been subject to bleeding for twelve years.* [26]*She had suffered a great deal under the care of many doctors and had spent all she had, yet instead of getting better she grew worse.* [27]*When she heard about Jesus, she came up behind him in the crowd and touched his cloak,* [28]*because she thought, "If I just touch his clothes, I will be healed."* [29]*Immediately her bleeding stopped and she felt in her body that she was freed from her suffering.*

[30]*At once Jesus realized that power had gone out from him. He turned around in the crowd and asked, "Who touched my clothes?"*

[31]*"You see the people crowding against you," his disciples answered, "and yet you can ask, 'Who touched me?'"*

[32]*But Jesus kept looking around to see who had done it.* [33]*Then the woman, knowing what had happened to her, came and fell at his feet and, trembling with fear, told him the whole truth.* [34]*He said to her, "Daughter, your faith has healed you. Go in peace and be freed from your suffering."*

# Group Questions

# Notes

Every group meeting has three parts: **(1) To Begin** (15 minutes) to break the ice; **(2) Read Scripture and Discuss** (30 Minutes); and **(3) To Close and Pray** (15–30 Minutes). Try to keep on schedule. The most important time is the prayer time.

## TO BEGIN / 15 Minutes (Choose 1 or 2)

❏ Who is the paramedic in your family—who is not squeamish about a little blood?
❏ Are you the type who would rather suffer with pain than go see a doctor?
❏ How do you feel when you are crowded into an elevator or subway?

## READ SCRIPTURE AND DISCUSS / 30 Minutes

❏ What makes you think that the woman was desperate when she approached Jesus?
❏ What was the woman risking when she reached out and touched Jesus? (see Notes for verse 5:25)
❏ Why do you think Jesus made the sick woman reveal herself?
❏ Why was this woman healed when nobody else in the crowd was healed?
❏ Was this healing strictly physical? Or emotional as well? Or relational? Or vocational?
❏ What did it cost Jesus to be involved in this woman's life?
❏ When is the last time you felt desperate enough to reach out to God—at the risk of ridicule and humiliation—for help in your life?
❏ What is the role of Jesus in healing today? Of faith? Of prayer?

## TO CLOSE AND PRAY / 15–30 Minutes

❏ If your body could talk, what would your body tell you about the stress in your life?
❏ What do you appreciate most about this group?
❏ How can this group pray for you this week?

**Summary.** We now come to the third healing which we will examine. In this account we see Jesus deal with a long-standing medical problem that had persisted for years, that had been untreatable by doctors, and which had both physical and social consequences for the woman involved. In it we see anew Jesus' awesome power; we get new insight into the role of faith in healing; and we discover the kind of whole-person healing that Jesus brings that restores not only the body but the psyche and the spirit.

This story is told by Mark as the third of four "power" stories by which he introduces unit two of his Gospel (4:35–6:30). Up to this point in time the disciples have assumed that Jesus is merely a great teacher. He does what teachers do: have disciples, teach, heal, and cast out demons. In these four stories they discover that he is substantially more than just a great teacher. They see his power over nature when he stills the storm in Mark 4:35–41 (which we will study in Unit 9). They see his power over the vilest of evil when he casts out a legion of demons from a man in Mark 5:1–20 (which we will study in Unit 6). They see his power over death itself when he raises a young girl from the dead in Mark 5:21–24a; 35–43. Here they see his power over chronic illness as he heals this woman who merely touches the hem of his garment.

This incident is actually sandwiched between the opening and conclusion of the story of Jairus' daughter (5:21–24; 35–43). Thus, the two stories are interwoven signifying that they are to be understood in relation to each other. Both deal with females who were second class citizens in the first-century scheme of things; both women are unclean (the one due to her interminable menstrual flow, the other because she had died); both are confronted by desperate situations which lead to death; and both women are healed by faith through Jesus' touch.

**5:25** *a woman was there.* While on the way to Jairus' home to see his dying daughter, this woman, part of the crowd following after Jesus to see what he could do for Jairus' daughter, approached him in secret. She should not have been there in the crowd. Because of the nature of her illness she was considered "unclean." If people touched her, they too would become "unclean" and be rendered unable to participate in ceremonial worship until they went through a prescribed cleansing ritual.

**subject to bleeding.** This was probably a steady hemorrhaging from her womb. Not only would this lead to obvious physical and emotional problems of weakness and sexual dysfunction, but such bleeding rendered her ritually impure (see Lev 15:25–30), cutting her off from involvement in the religious life of her people. Since many people assumed that chronic problems like this were God's judgment upon a person for their sin, she undoubtedly experienced some measure of condemnation from others as well. As a result she has to seek out Jesus in this surreptitious way.

**5:26** When Luke the physician told this story (Luke 8:42–48) he dropped out this verse with its rather scathing condemnation of doctors! Mark's point is not to cast aspersions on the medical practitioners of his day, but to highlight the seriousness of the woman's condition. Like the demoniac in the previous story, this woman was beyond human help. She had exhausted all her resources in the attempt to find help but to no avail.

**the care of many doctors.** Typical cures would have included such things as carrying the ash of an ostrich egg in a certain cloth or drinking wine mixed with rubber, alum, and garden crocuses.

**5:28 If I just touch his clothes, I will be healed.** Jesus' reputation as a healer had obviously preceded him. Yet the woman's perception of Jesus at this point was probably that he was some type of magician who possessed remarkable powers that would be transferred to whatever objects touched him. There is no attempt on her part to establish genuine contact with Jesus: she simply wants to brush up against him so that she can be brought in contact with his power.

**5:29 Immediately.** This was a real miracle. Then and there she was healed, and she knew it.

**5:30 power.** This is the creative, mysterious, healing power of God.

**5:31 You see the people crowding against you.** And yet you can ask, 'Who touched me?' As in 4:38, the disciples fail to understand Jesus or what he is about. They can only see that his stopping to ask what seems to be a foolish question is wasting the limited time they have to get to Jairus' house before his daughter dies. In the press of the crowd, undoubt-

edly many people were touching him, yet Jesus was a aware that a special work had been done for one person and he desired to know who that was.

**5:32** Jesus insists that the person who touched him reveal herself. At first glance this seems to be a cruel question since Jesus forces this woman—who should not have been there in the first place and who had a disease she probably would not have wanted to talk about publically—to identify herself. However, her healing will not be complete without this since her illness had not only physical but emotional and social consequences. In the same way that he insisted that the leper go through the cleansing ritual and thus be admitted back into society (1:44), here Jesus makes it publically known that she has been healed so that she can once again have a normal social life. In other words, he healed her both physically and socially.

**5:33 trembling with fear.** Fear is a common element in all these four power stories (4:40–41; 5:15; 5:36). Not only do the people in the scenes face frightening circumstances, but there is fear before Jesus. Everyone is caught off guard, as well, by his authority that exceeds all their expectations. This woman may have feared that she had done something wrong; she may have feared that Jesus would shame her in front of everyone; she may have feared that her healing would be revoked.

**5:34 Daughter.** This word changes everything. It stresses that she is indeed a child of God, loved and not under his judgment. It affirms that she is no longer a social outcast, but is in community with the other children of God. It establishes a personal relationship of care between Jesus and her that is in stark contrast to the impersonal, magical notions with which she may have approached him.

**your faith has healed you.** It was her faith that impelled her to reach out to Jesus—the source of healing power. The word Jesus uses to tell her that she is healed comes from the same root as the words "salvation" and "Savior." Spiritual as well as physical healing is in view here.

**Go in peace.** Jesus did not mean by this "Be free from worry." This phrase means "Be complete, be whole."

# Notes

## Healing in the First Century

In the first century, healing was accomplished by three means: through medicine, by magic, or by miracle. Medicine involves diagnosis and prescription, much as it functions today. However, first century medicine was based on a primitive view of how the body functioned and a rudimentary understanding of drugs and surgery. Quacks were widespread. Pliny the Elder decries what has become of medicine. Physicians prescribe costly medications instead of widely available natural substances. They promise long life to those who will pay for it. He quotes Cato concerning physicians: "They are a most intuitous and untractable race ... They have conspired among themselves to murder all barbarians with their medicine; a profession which they exercise for lucre, in order that they win our confidence, and dispatch us all the more easily. Have nothing to do with physicians." One finds this same attitude (though not expressed so vehemently) in Mark 5:26 when the experience of the woman with chronic bleeding is described: "She had suffered a great deal under the care of many doctors and had spent all she had, yet instead of getting better she grew worse." Interestingly, this verse is not included in the account by Luke (who was a doctor)!

Magic involved techniques of incantation, spells, and formulae, as well as the use of magical apparatus and other paraphernalia. Pliny is no happier with magicians than he is with doctors. He calls them "fraudulent charlatans" when they assert the magical powers of the hyena: "a sure safeguard against miscarriage is an amulet of gazelle leather containing white flesh from a hyena's breast, seven hairs from a hyena and the genital organ of a stag...The extreme end of the hyena's intestine prevails against the injustice of leaders and potentates, brings in success to petitions and a happy issue to trials and lawsuits, if it is merely kept on the person." Rabbis, in their healing, sometimes verged on magic. For example, the Talmud describes how to deal with a fever. A knife made of iron is tied by a braid of hair to a thorn bush and on successive days verses from Exodus are repeated. Then a magic formula is pronounced and the cure is complete.

Miracle involved healing by the action of a god, either directly or through a chosen agent. Here the issue had to do with ways of getting on the good side of the god and the related problem of avoiding antagonizing the god or arousing the demons. That the gods could heal was not disputed; the question was how to get their attention and benevolence. In the hellenistic world, there were abundant healing shrines at which one could invoke the healing power of the gods. Within the Bible, Yahweh is seen as a powerful healer who worked through prophets, priests and teachers to heal his people.

Certainly healing was central to the ministry of Jesus. One fifth of the stories in the first three Gospels describe or allude to healing or exorcism. In the Gospel of John, four of the seven "signs" involve healing.

# UNIT 4—A Man With Leprosy / Mark 1:40–45

## Scripture

A Man With Leprosy

[40]*A man with leprosy*[a] *came to him and begged him on his knees, "If you are willing, you can make me clean."*

[41]*Filled with compassion, Jesus reached out his hand and touched the man. "I am willing," he said. "Be clean!"* [42]*Immediately the leprosy left him and he was cured.*

[43]*Jesus sent him away at once with a strong warning:* [44]*"See that you don't tell this to anyone. But go, show yourself to the priest and offer the sacrifices that Moses commanded for your cleansing, as a testimony to them."* [45]*Instead he went out and began to talk freely, spreading the news. As a result, Jesus could no longer enter a town openly but stayed outside in lonely places. Yet the people still came to him from everywhere.*

[a]40 The Greek word was used for various diseases affecting the skin—not necessarily leprosy.

# Group Questions

**TO BEGIN / 15 Minutes** (Choose 1 or 2)

❑ Have you ever been quarantined at home because you had an infectious disease?
❑ What kind of people do you resist touching?
❑ Who are the social outcasts and "lepers" in your town?

**READ SCRIPTURE AND DISCUSS / 30 Minutes**

❑ Reading between the lines, how do you think the leper was feeling when he approached Jesus? (See Note on this page for "leprosy.")
❑ What was the leper really saying in his statement to Jesus: "If you are willing, you can make me clean"?
❑ What was Jesus risking when he reached out and touched him? What would the people in the crowd think?
❑ When the leper was "cured," what would this mean in his everyday life?
❑ In the movie *Ben Hur*, leprosy was used to symbolize the deeper "miracle" of transformation when the mother and sister of Ben Hur were healed at the same moment that the crucifixion occurred. Do you see any deeper meaning in this story?
❑ What is the closest you have come to feeling like a "leper"? Who reached out to you and "touched" you?
❑ Who are the people you invite over for dinner or reach out to on a regular basis? Who do you not reach out to?
❑ Who are the people your church reaches out to? Who would feel uncomfortable in your church because they would be looked down on?

**TO CLOSE AND PRAY / 15–30 Minutes**

❑ What would it take for you to reach out and invite a new person to this group next week?
❑ What is keeping you from sharing some of your own hurts in this group?
❑ How can this group help you in prayer this week?

# Notes

**Summary.** In the final healing that we will examine, we see Jesus curing one of the most dread diseases in the first-century: leprosy. Leprosy was considered to be one of the worst diseases to befall a person—a kind of living death. Jesus once again does battle with the power of evil (since disease is a form of possession by Satan). The early church used stories such as this one as illustrations of how Jesus has come to free people from sin. Leprosy serves as a particularly apt illustration of sin and evil. Like sin, it brings progressive physical and psychological disintegration, it disfigures both body and soul, it alienates people from one another, it leads those it infects to despise their own selves, and it cuts people off from the worship of God (since lepers were forbidden from coming to the temple). Perhaps most tragically, like sin it was beyond one's ability to change. This miracle implies that in the presence of Jesus, sin, like this man's leprosy, no longer has the final word about a person's destiny.

**1:40 *leprosy.*** No disease was dreaded more than leprosy. It brought not only physical disfigurement but, because of fear of contamination, social banishment as well. It is important to note, however, that the word leprosy was used in the first century to describe a variety of skin diseases (including such things as psoriasis and even ring-worm) and not just what is now known to be true leprosy (Hansen's disease). Whatever the specific skin disease this man had, it was an awful disease since it caused him to be banished from contact with others. OT law required that lepers dwell alone outside the camp; that they cover the lower part of their faces; and that they must go about in torn clothes crying out "Unclean, unclean!" to warn away others (Lev 13:45–46). However, in Jesus' day lepers were prohibited only from living in Jerusalem and a few other ancient cities. Although lepers could live where they wanted, they were considered religiously unclean. Thus, the rabbis developed elaborate regulations regarding how they were to be avoided in order to maintain one's ritual purity. This underlined their social isolation and sense of self-hatred.

***came to him.*** What the leper did was forbidden by law. The leper should have sought to avoid drawing near Jesus so as not to render him religiously unclean. The rabbis taught that if a leper passed by a clean man, the clean man would not become unclean. However, if the leper stopped, then the clean man would become unclean.

*If you are willing, you can make me clean.*
Whether through actually seeing Jesus perform healings (1:32–34) or through hearing reports of his ability, the leper has a clear, strong faith in Jesus' power to heal. His only concern is whether Jesus would be willing to do so or not, probably a reflection on the leper's terribly crushed self-esteem.

**1:41** *Filled with compassion.* Human suffering evoked a deep, affective response from Jesus. He was not afraid of strong emotions.

*reached out his hand and touched the man.*
Actually touching a leper was unimaginable to most first century people. Not only did one risk contracting the disease but such contact made the healthy person ritually impure and thus unable to participate in the religious life of the community. By this gesture, Jesus showed his lack of concern for the details of religious tradition when they came into conflict with human need. From the leper's perspective, the effect of Jesus' touch must have been overwhelming. He had undoubtedly come to think of himself as untouchable and unlovable. This touch affirmed him as a fellow human in spite of his disease.

**1:42** *Immediately.* This is a favorite word for Mark. In this context it shows the immediacy and efficacy of Jesus' word. It is reminiscent of the word of God in creation as seen in Genesis 1 in which "and God said …" is immediately followed by "… and it was so."

**1:43** *Jesus sent him away at once with a strong warning.* The NSRV has "after sternly warning him" which better captures the note of harshness and rebuke implied in the word used here. The stern charge was to prevent what did indeed end up happening. The man did tell others resulting in Jesus' inability to continue his preaching ministry as he had intended.

*at once.* This is the same word translated in verse 42 as "immediately." It emphasizes Jesus' decisive, urgent action.

**1:44** *don't tell this to anyone.* Jesus constantly urges those who have experienced dramatic healing not to tell others. On the surface this appears to be strange behavior. Didn't Jesus want to get out the message of who he was? The problem was that first-century Jews, fueled by the vivid, highly nationalistic, apocalyptic literature (written in the period following

the close of the OT and prior to the NT), expected a bloody, militaristic Messiah who would rid them from the yoke of the hated Romans. Seeing evidences of Jesus' power, such as the healing of a leper, would cause people to see him as that sort of Messiah. Hence this could precipitate a tragic revolt against Rome. This very attitude is reported in John 6:14–15, following the feeding of the 5000. The people wanted to make Jesus King. Jesus, however, withdrew into the hills to prevent this from happening. Jesus was the Messiah but not the kind of Messiah that was expected. He needed time to communicate what kind of Messiah he was (he came to die not to conquer by force). Eventually the time for secrecy will be over, but at this early point in his ministry he did not want to rouse false hopes that would make his true mission difficult.

*offer the sacrifices that Moses commanded.* In Leviticus 14:1–32 the ritual is outlined whereby a leper is declared "clean." Such certification was vital to a leper: it was that person's way back into human society.

*as a testimony to them.* This refers to the priests. Since they were the ones who had to verify a person's cleansing, they would have made an official pronouncement of his healing. Thus, the healing would have been a testimony in two senses. Positively, it would be clear evidence that God was indeed at work in and through Jesus. The rabbis considered curing leprosy as difficult as raising someone from the dead (in the OT, only Moses and Elisha ever successfully cured someone of leprosy). If the priests acknowledged that Jesus had indeed cured this man's leprosy, it would have been a powerful evidence to them of his divine authority. Negatively, if the priests refused to acknowledge Jesus' authority even after validating this remarkable healing, then the healing would be a witness against them in the Day of Judgment since they had seen irrefutable evidence of God's work through him yet still resisted his teaching.

**1:45** *talk freely; spreading the news.* Jesus' command was ignored. The leper's joy could not be contained as he told everyone how he came to be healed. The terms used here are common words used later on in the NT to describe the nature and content of Christian preaching. While the man was not to have done so at this time, he does serve as an example of a Christian witness who proclaims the good news of Christ to all.

# Notes

***Jesus could no longer enter a town openly.*** His teaching ministry (1:38) was hindered by the clamor of people coming to him only for exorcisms and healings. While they were a sign of what he had come to do, his real mission was to pronounce the deliverance from sin for those who would repent and seek after the kingdom of God (1:15; 2:17).

***lonely places.*** Mark began this cycle of stories with Jesus emerging from the wilderness in order to start his ministry (Mark 1:14–15). This section ends with him back in a place of isolation, driven there by the disobedience of the leper (understandable though it may be) and thus hindered in his Galilean ministry.

***the people still came to him.*** This is the point which Mark wants to make in this opening description of Jesus' ministry: Jesus is immensely popular with the common people. In his next section (2:1–3:6), Mark will show that, in contrast, he was not at all popular with the religious leaders.

## The Healing Power of Jesus

It is clear that Jesus has the power to heal disease of all sorts. We have seen him heal blindness, paralysis, chronic menstrual bleeding, and even leprosy. Elsewhere in the New Testament he cures a fever (Mark 1:29–31), gives speech to a mute (Matt 9:32–34), restores the use of a withered hand (Mark 3:1–6), heals a man with dropsy (swelling due to the accumulation of fluids—Luke 14:1–6), replaces an ear that has been cut off (Luke 22:49–51), and restores speech and hearing to a deaf-mute (Mark 7:31–37).

How did he do it? Was the healing Jesus did purely psychosomatic in nature? That is, did he heal the mind which, in turn, cured the body? This might have been the case in certain instances. Modern medicine has clearly established the fact that there is a mind-body link.

But in other instances, Jesus quite clearly effects organic change. The damaged spine of the paralytic was repaired so he could walk (Mark 2:1–12). The fever of Peter's mother-in-law not only broke with the healing touch of Jesus, but she was able to get up immediately and suffered none of the usual weakness which follows the passing of a fever (Mark 1:29–31). And ears simply do not grow back with a touch as they did for the high priest's servant (Luke 22:49–51).

But what about today? Does Jesus still heal? The answer has to be "Yes." Many people can testify to healing as a result of prayer, and not all of these cures can be construed to be pyscho-somatic in nature. But it is also clear that not everyone who prays is healed. Furthermore, it is clear that all faith-healing is temporary in nature. In the end, everybody dies.

What, then, can we say about healing today? Only that we can and should pray for healing, with the faith that we are granted, knowing that God does still heal but knowing also that God is sovereign and answers prayer as he will (James 5:13–16). Whatever the outcome of our prayers we rest securely in the hands of a loving God who cares for us more deeply than anyone else possibly can.

# UNIT 5—Jesus Drives Out an Evil Spirit / Mark 1:21–28

## Scripture

Jesus Drives Out an Evil Spirit

<sup>21</sup>*They went to Capernaum, and when the Sabbath came, Jesus went into the synagogue and began to teach.* <sup>22</sup>*The people were amazed at his teaching, because he taught them as one who had authority, not as the teachers of the law.* <sup>23</sup>*Just then a man in their synagogue who was possessed by an evil*<sup>a</sup> *spirit cried out,* <sup>24</sup>*"What do you want with us, Jesus of Nazareth? Have you come to destroy us? I know who you are— the Holy One of God!"*

<sup>25</sup>*"Be quiet!" said Jesus sternly. "Come out of him!"* <sup>26</sup>*The evil spirit shook the man violently and came out of him with a shriek.*

<sup>27</sup>*The people were all so amazed that they asked each other, "What is this? A new teaching—and with authority! He even gives orders to evil spirits and they obey him."* <sup>28</sup>*News about him spread quickly over the whole region of Galilee.*

<sup>a</sup>23 Greek [*unclean*]; also in verses 26 and 27

# Group Questions

**TO BEGIN / 15 Minutes** (Choose 1 or 2)

❑ Have you ever known someone who practiced "demon worship" or "spiritism" (or ever visited a foreign country where this type of spiritism was practiced)?

❑ How do you feel about Quija boards, tarot cards, palm readers and horoscopes?

**READ SCRIPTURE AND DISCUSS / 30 Minutes**

❑ How would you describe the person in this story who was "possessed by an evil spirit"? (See Note on the next page for "an evil spirit.") Do you think this person had two personalities ... or was he possessed by an outside force?

❑ What do you learn about demons from this episode in the synagogue?

❑ Why would Jesus order the demon in this person to "Be silent"?

❑ The word "authority" is used to describe Jesus' teaching style. What else does this passage teach about Jesus' authority?

❑ Have you seen or known of anyone who seemed to be "possessed" by an evil spirit? Do you think a Christian can be "possessed" by an evil spirit and the Holy Spirit at the same time?

❑ Do you think a Christian can be attacked by an evil spirit? What protection does the Christian have against such attacks?

❑ What is the relationship between demon possession and mind-altering drugs?

❑ Do you believe in exorcism (casting out demons)?

**TO CLOSE AND PRAY / 15–30 Minutes**

❑ On a scale from 1 to 10, how much authority does Jesus Christ have over your life? What would he have to cast out of your life to rate a 10?

❑ Is your group a place where miracles are possible and expected?

❑ What miracle would you ask this group to pray about for you?

# Notes

**Summary.** Now we turn our attention to Jesus' power over evil forces. The next two accounts deal with exorcism: the casting out of demons who had possessed human beings. While healing by faith is familiar to us in the twentieth century, for many people casting out demons is strange business indeed. In fact, in the first century, healing and exorcism were often lumped together. When the people flock to Jesus in Capernaum after the exorcism in the synagogue which we will study in this unit, the text says: "That evening after sunset the people brought to Jesus all the sick and demon-possessed. The whole town gathered at the door, and Jesus healed many who had various diseases. He also drove out many demons ..." (Mark 1:32–34). Exorcism was a kind of healing. The first-century person would have been hard-put to distinguish always between maladies caused by disease and those caused by demons. Healers were often also exorcists.

The account we are going to examine is the first public act of ministry recorded in the Gospel of Mark. Jesus appears on the sabbath in the synagogue at Capernaum with his four newly appointed disciples. Here, with God's chosen people assembled, Jesus makes his presence known by the quality of his teaching and by his extraordinary power over demons.

The question which his actions raise for the people was this: Who is this man? Given their limited experience of Jesus at this point in time they probably would have answered: He is a great teacher. What he does here is what teachers do: gather disciples (he now has four), teach, cast out demons, and heal (1:29–34). This was the work of rabbis in the first century. However, Jesus sets himself apart from other rabbis by his extraordinary effectiveness— his teaching was authoritative and his exorcism was effective. Few other teachers could say this.

**1:21 *Capernaum*.** This was a town on the north end of the Sea of Galilee, three miles west of the River Jordan. It was a center of the fishing industry and the site of a custom's post.

***synagogue.*** In first century Israel, the temple in Jerusalem was the sole site for sacrifices and was attended by numerous priests and other officials. In contrast, there were synagogues in each population center which people attended each week for worship and instruction. Synagogues were run by lay committees with no professional clergy attached to them.

# Notes (Continued)

Anyone could speak as long as he had permission from the leaders.

**1:22 *amazed.*** Throughout the Gospel of Mark, Jesus' words and actions provoke amazement and surprise among the people. Neither his word nor his actions were customary—they could not be easily integrated with what went on day by day. Here was something new that challenged accepted ways of thinking and living. Jesus' words and actions were pointers to the kingdom he was establishing, a kingdom that called for a response of repentance and faith from those wishing to be part of it (Mark 1:15).

***at his teaching.*** Compared to the other Gospels, Mark does not record a lot of Jesus' teaching. There are two major sections: Mark 4:1–34 and Mark 13. In the fourth unit of Mark (8:31–10:52) there are various brief teaching sections concerning the nature of discipleship. His central message as recorded in this Gospel is summed up in 1:15: "The kingdom of God is near. Repent and believe the good news."

***he taught them as one who had authority, not as the teachers of the law.*** The teachers of the Law were men schooled in the interpretation of the Law and responsible for helping the people in general understand and apply the Law to their situations. Their authority lay in their ability to quote the teachings of previous rabbis on the subject at hand. In contrast, Jesus taught directly. An example is seen in Matthew's version of the Sermon on the Mount in which Jesus counters traditional teaching with his repeated statement, "But I tell you ..." (Mt 5:22, 28, 32,34,39,44) without the use of quotes from earlier rabbis to back him up.

**1:23 *an evil spirit.*** The Gospels frequently refer to these malignant, supernatural beings, able to harm and even possess people. We are not told what manifestation this spirit exhibited in this man's life, but from other stories in the NT we learn that a demonic spirit's activity can range from giving people a supernatural ability to foresee the future (Acts 16:16) to leading people to destructive, violent behaviors (Mark 5:1–5; 9:17). The reality of evil spirits was widely acknowledged in the ancient world (as well as in most parts of the world today that have not become closed to the reality of the supernatural). The Biblical understanding is that such spirits were Satan's legions who joined with him in the ancient revolt against God. While not all sickness nor bizarre behavior was attributed to the work of evil spirits, such ailments were thought to be common manifestations of possession by a spirit. Given their prominence in the Gospels in contrast to their relative absence elsewhere in the Bible, it seems that their activity is especially exposed in the light of the presence of Jesus. In overcoming this evil spirit, Jesus demonstrated his power over Satan. He has come to bind the strong man (Mark 3:27), freeing people for God. The kingdom of God will be marked by the absence of such destructive forces. This is the opening encounter in what would be an on-going battle.

**1:24 *What do you want with us.*** At first the evil spirit is defiant and resistant.

***I know who you are.*** By identifying Jesus, first using his human name and then by his divine title, the demon was relying on ancient magical practices in the hope of gaining mastery over Jesus. It was believed that knowledge of a person's true identity (or secret name) gave one power over that person. Since the demon named Jesus, supposedly he would have Jesus in his power. However, such a tactic did not work with Jesus!

***the Holy One of God.*** The evil spirit recognizes Jesus for who he is—the divine Son of God. In contrast, it will be quite some time before anyone else, including the disciples, understands this.

**1:25 *Be quiet!*** Far from being overcome by the demon's ability to name him, Jesus orders the demon to be silent. This is yet another way in which Jesus asserts his authority over the demon. Throughout the Gospels, Jesus does not allow the demons to bear witness to him. The problem he seeks to avoid is similar to the problem which is raised when those who are healed miraculously (as, for example, the leper in the last unit) witness to this fact. People might jump to the wrong conclusion. They might acclaim Jesus Messiah and flock to his cause, expecting him to strike out at Rome when, in fact, he had come to die. Besides, Jesus does not need demonic witness to reveal who he is. In Mark's Gospel, up until the end of the story, only the narrator and the demons know that Jesus is the "Holy One of God." It takes the whole of Mark's Gospel for Jesus' disciples to realize this fact!

***sternly.*** Literally, this is "he rebuked him." The same word is used in Mark 4:39 when Jesus orders the tumult of the sea and wind to be still. The intent of the word is to show Jesus as the one who has authority to control and restrain the forces leading to chaos.

**Come out of him!** In Jesus' day there were exorcists who used a combination of religious and magical practices to try to release people whose personality had been invaded and warped by an evil spirit. It was an elaborate, mysterious process with a questionable success rate. In contrast, Jesus issues a simple word of command which is immediately obeyed.

**1:26 came out of him.** Where did the spirit go? According to Jude 6, Christ's judgment upon such spirits is to bind them unto the Day of Judgment at which time they will experience the judgment of Hell. In spite of popular thought, Hell is not the realm where Satan and his demons are in charge: the NT pictures it as the place of their everlasting torment.

**1:27 amazed.** See Note on verse 22. The amazement here is not over the presence of the man with a demon in their midst since that would not have been an unexpected phenomenon for people aware of and open to spiritual reality. What amazed them was Jesus' power over the demon. Such amazement contains not only joy but some alarm and even fear. Who is this man who possesses such unsuspected power?

**1:28 News about him spread.** The people had witnessed amazing power and heard extraordinary teaching and so it is not at all surprising that they told everyone they met what had happened in the synagogue. Jesus' power over the spirits led him to become a sought-after person in the region (see Mark 1:32; 2:1; 3:11).

## Are Evil Spirits Still At Work?

Is it credible in a secularized, scientific, materialistic society to draw any meaning from a story about Jesus' power over evil spirits? Aren't evil spirits simply a way that pre-scientific people explained things like disease, insanity, epilepsy, and personality disorders?

It is unquestionably true that the modern understanding of physical and psychological processes has helped countless people who in an earlier day would have experienced enormous suffering (and perhaps rejection). Yet it is sheer cultural prejudice to assume that modern society has a complete grasp on all the dynamics that affect human behavior. While an earlier day saw people go too far in attributing unpleasant or destructive tendencies to the work of spirits, has not our society gone too far in ruling out the presence of the supernatural entirely? The Bible assumes a whole realm of spiritual entities that affect humanity in a variety of ways, but it does not attribute all sickness or hardship directly to such a source (see 1Ti 5:23).

Richard Lovelace, a church historian, uses an analogy of sickness to describe the Biblical perspective on the influence of demons in human affairs. Sickness can be caused by poor habits (such as smoking), bacteria and viruses, and external forces (like toxic wastes). The treatment of various health problems has to match their cause. Likewise, the Bible pictures human behavior as being affected by physical and psychological factors, social and cultural circumstances, and demonic activity (the germs of the cosmos!). As with health issues, problems in human behavior have to be treated in accord with their source. One Malaysian Christian commented that the main reason his friends were drawn to Jesus was that it was clear that he had power to free them from the domination of the spirits that so affected their lives. Rather than allowing our sense of reality to be formed only by the limited experience of our culture, we might do better to allow it to be shaped as well by the Scripture and the experience of people in other cultures.

# UNIT 6—The Healing of a Demon-Possessed Man / Mark 5:1–20

## Scripture

The Healing of a Demon-Possessed Man

**5** *They went across the lake to the region of the Gerasenes.*[a] *²When Jesus got out of the boat, a man with an evil*[b] *spirit came from the tombs to meet him. ³This man lived in the tombs, and no one could bind him any more, not even with a chain. ⁴For he had often been chained hand and foot, but he tore the chains apart and broke the irons on his feet. No one was strong enough to subdue him. ⁵Night and day among the tombs and in the hills he would cry out and cut himself with stones.*

*⁶When he saw Jesus from a distance, he ran and fell on his knees in front of him. ⁷He shouted at the top of his voice, "What do you want with me, Jesus, Son of the Most High God? Swear to God that you won't torture me!" ⁸For Jesus had said to him, "Come out of this man, you evil spirit!"*

*⁹Then Jesus asked him, "What is your name?" "My name is Legion," he replied, "for we are many." ¹⁰And he begged Jesus again and again not to send them out of the area.*

*¹¹A large herd of pigs was feeding on the nearby hillside. ¹²The demons begged Jesus, "Send us among the pigs; allow us to go into them." ¹³He gave them permission, and the evil spirits came out and went into the pigs. The herd, about two thousand in number, rushed down the steep bank into the lake and were drowned.*

*¹⁴Those tending the pigs ran off and reported this in the town and countryside, and the people went out to see what had happened. ¹⁵When they came to Jesus, they saw the man who had been possessed by the legion of demons, sitting there, dressed and in his right mind; and they were afraid. ¹⁶Those who had seen it told the people what had happened to the demon-possessed man—and told about the pigs as well. ¹⁷Then the people began to plead with Jesus to leave their region. ¹⁸As Jesus was getting into the boat, the man who had been demon-possessed begged to go with him. ¹⁹Jesus did not let him, but said, "Go home to your family and tell them how much the Lord has done for you, and how he has had mercy on you." ²⁰So the man went away and began to tell in the Decapolis*[c] *how much Jesus had done for him. And all the people were amazed.*

[a]1 Some manuscripts *Gadarenes*; other manuscripts *Gergesenes*
[b]2 Greek *unclean*; also in verses 8 and 13   [c]20 That is, the Ten Cities

# Group Questions

## TO BEGIN / 15 Minutes (Choose 1 or 2)

❏ Growing up, where did your family go for vacation?

❏ What vacation do you especially remember because of a terrible thing that happened?

❏ What is guaranteed to ruin a nice vacation for you now? Bad weather? Disappointing lodging? Unexpected detours?

## READ SCRIPTURE AND DISCUSS / 30 Minutes

❏ The scene opens with Jesus taking his disciples on a boat trip for a little rest. How do you think the disciples felt when they arrived on the other shore and found this mad man?

❏ What are some clues in the first paragraph that this man was no ordinary man? How would a psychiatrist diagnose this man?

❏ What is the difference between the demon possession in this story and the demon possession in the last study (page 26)?

❏ In the interplay between the demon and Jesus in verses 9–13, what do you learn about demons?

❏ If you were a doctor, how would you describe the change that came over the man when the demons left him?

❏ How did the town react when they heard the news? If you could put in a good word for the pig farmers, what would you say?

❏ Have you ever been caught in a conflict of interest like the pig farmers in the story—where your pocketbook prevented you from rejoicing at the change God brought?

## TO CLOSE AND PRAY / 15–30 Minutes

❏ Do you ever long to see miracles like this and radical change happen in your town?

❏ If you could ask God for a miracle in your church, what would it be?

❏ How can this group pray for a miracle in your own life this week?

# Notes

**Summary.** We now examine a second exorcism. This time Jesus confronts a man who is ravished by not one but thousands of demons. This is the ultimate in possession. Once again Jesus demonstrates his power by casting out this combined force of demons and healing a man whose body and personality had been overwhelmed by their evil possession.

This is the second of the four "power" stories by which the disciples come to understand that Jesus is no mere teacher. (See the Summary section in Unit 3, p. 19, for more details about the structure of Mark 4:35–5:43.)

**5:1 *They went across the lake.*** Jesus and his disciples were in a boat on the Sea of Galilee. This incident takes place after Jesus calms the fierce storm that threatened to swamp their boat (Mark 4:35–41). Given the fact that Jesus and the 12 left the Capernaum side of the lake "when evening came" (4:35) by the time they arrive at the other side it is probably dark.

***the lake.*** This was the Sea of Galilee, a deep, freshwater lake, 13 miles long and eight miles at it widest point. It was pear-shaped and ringed by mountains, though open at its north and south ends. Fierce winds blew into this bowl-shaped sea creating savage and unpredictable storms, one of which Jesus and the 12 had just experienced.

***the region of the Gerasenes.*** The precise location of their landing is not clear. However, it is on the other side of the lake from Capernaum, in Gentile territory, probably near the lower end of the Sea of Galilee.

**5:2 *Jesus got out of the boat.*** No mention is made of the disciples in this story. Given what they had been through in the storm on the Sea of Galilee (4:35–41—see Unit 11) and the fact that they landed in a Gentile region at night in a graveyard with a nightmare-like figure howling at them, it is not surprising that only Jesus seems to have gotten out of the boat to face this terror.

***a man with an evil spirit.*** There was wide-spread belief that demons could enter and take control of a person's body; speaking and acting through that person. First-century people lived in dread of demons. Thus they avoided places, like cemeteries, where demons were thought to dwell. The demons were understood to be Satan's legions. In overcoming

# Notes (Continued)

them, Jesus was demonstrating his power over Satan and his work.

**1:3–5** The picture painted of this man was that of a living terror: He was naked, physically he was so powerful he could not be subdued, he was cut-up and perhaps bleeding, and he cried out in great distress living there among the tombs.

**1:6–9** The naming-ritual begins and the demons try to master Jesus by crying out his true identity (see Note for 1:24, p. 31). All the while Jesus is commanding the demons to leave the man (v. 8). Finally, Jesus with his superior power compels the demons to reveal their name (v. 9).

**1:7 Son of the Most High God.** The disciples asked in the previous story who Jesus is (Mark 4:41) and the demon-filled man, with supernatural insight, here points out his divine nature. Interestingly, this title is how God was often referred to by Gentiles (see Ge 14:18–24; Da 4:17).

**Swear to God that you won't torture me!** It is not clear what they feared. According to Jewish apocalyptic literature, the torment of demons was to take place at the time of the final judgment. Jesus' presence signals to them the beginning of the end-times.

**1:9 Legion.** The name for a company consisting of 6000 Roman soldiers. The man was occupied not by one but by a huge number of demons. This name also conveys the sense of warfare that is going on between Jesus and Satan. The Roman legions were the first-century world's most fierce fighting force. As such it is an apt name for the kind of overwhelmingly powerful possession by evil that had occurred. Even in this ultimate situation, Jesus demonstrates his power over evil. It cannot stand against him even in its most virulent form.

**1:10** Again, it is not clear what they feared. Perhaps they feared being banished to Hell. Contrary to popular thought, Hell is not the realm where Satan and his demons are in charge. The NT pictures it as the place of their torment. According to Jude 6, Christ would bind such disobedient spirits until the day of judgment. Nor is it clear that being allowed to enter the pigs—who were quickly drowned—was all that more desirable. The fact that they entered into pigs reveals their unclean, corrupt natures.

**1:11 pigs.** This was a Gentile herd. No Jew would raise pigs since they were considered unclean animals (Lev 11:1–8). For a Jew to eat or touch a pig meant that he or she was defiled and thus unable to participate in worship until a ceremonial cleansing was performed. This was probably a herd made up of pigs owned by various people in town.

**1:13 rushed down the steep bank.** The stampede of the herd gave evidence that the demons had, indeed, been driven out of the man. Their mad suicidal rush to the sea shows what kind of creatures they are. Their destructive impact on the pigs is in sharp contrast to the peace and healing Jesus brought to the demoniac.

**1:14–17** The incident is reported to the townspeople who arrive in mass and find not only the drowned pigs but the healed demoniac.

**1:15 they were afraid.** It might be expected that they would rejoice that this man who had terrorized them and whom they could no longer restrain was now healed. But instead they are fearful of Jesus, who has the power to overcome the demons and destroy their town herd.

**1:17 the people began to plead with Jesus to leave.** They want no part of one who in their eyes would appear to be a powerful magician; or who regarded a single mad man to be worth more than their whole town herd.

**1:18–20** The focus shifts from the frightened townfolk to the grateful ex-demoniac. He wants to join Jesus' band but is instead commanded to return home and share his story of God's mercy.

**1:19 tell.** In contrast to what Jesus said to the leper: "See that you don't tell this to anyone," (Mark 1:44, Unit 4), he wants this man to share the story of his healing. The difference is that the leper was Jewish and his story might cause people to think that the Messiah had come before they knew what kind of Messiah Jesus was. Gentiles, however, did not have such messianic expectations. Interestingly, what the ex-demoniac could tell them was limited. He could explain what he was like before he met Jesus, what had happened to him when he encountered Jesus and what little he knew about Jesus. This first Gentile witness to Jesus had no theological training; he sim-

## ARE YOU FEELING A LITTLE
# NERVOUS ABOUT BEING IN A SMALL GROUP?

**SYMPTOMS:** Do you break out into a sweat at the mention of small groups. Does your mouth turn to sawdust when it comes "your turn" to share? To pray?

**PRESCRIPTION:** Take this test to see if you are ready to belong to a small group. If you answer "yes" on seven out of ten questions below, you are probably ready to take the plunge.

1. Are you looking for a place where you can deal with the serious questions in your life right now?　☐ Yes　☐ No

2. Are you open to the possibility that God has something special for your life?
☐ Yes　☐ No

3. Are you open to the Bible as the source where God's will for your life can be explored?
☐ Yes　☐ No

4. Are you able to admit that you do not have all the answers about the Bible? God? Your own life?　☐ Yes　☐ No

5. Are you able to let others have questions about the Bible or God?　☐ Yes　☐ No

6. Are you willing to accept people in the group that are "Prodigal Sons" and have a long way to go in their spiritual faith?　☐ Yes　☐ No

7. Are you willing to keep anything that is shared in this group in strict confidence?　☐ Yes　☐ No

8. Are you willing to share in the responsibility for the group and to support group members with your prayers?　☐ Yes　☐ No

9. Are you willing to give priority to this group for a short period of time (such as six to twelve weeks) and consider making a longer commitment after this time?
☐ Yes　☐ No

10. Are you excited about the possibilities of belonging to a group that could make a difference in your life?　☐ Yes　☐ No

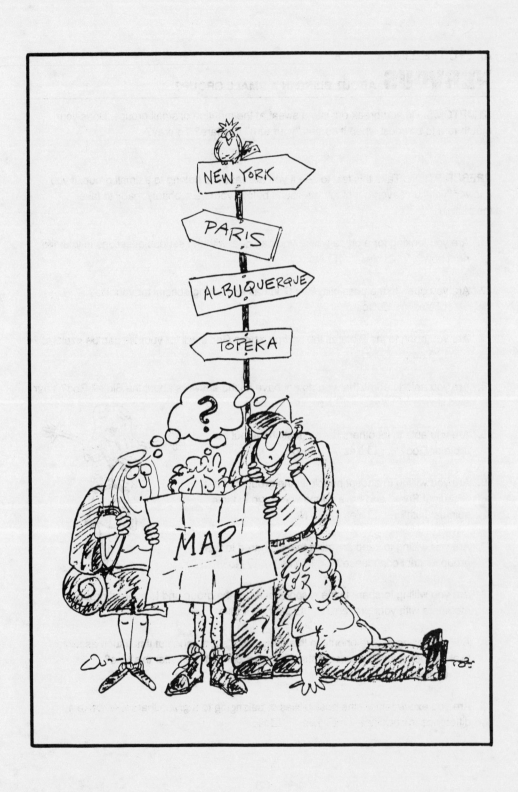

**ARE YOU FEELING A LITTLE**

# CONFUSED ABOUT YOUR PURPOSE?

**SYMPTOMS:** Do you feel like you are playing on a team that doesn't have any rules? Any direction? Any idea of what you want to do or accomplish? Or where you are going?

**PRESCRIPTION:** Before you ever started the group, you should have decided on a COVENANT that spelled out your purpose, rules, expectations, etc. If you didn't, call "time out" and decide *together* on a covenant.

Here's how. Take the first sentence below and ask everyone to finish the sentence. Then, try to come up with a one sentence statement that you all can agree to. "The purpose of our group is . . ."

Then, take the second sentence and decide on your specific goals, etc. . . . until you have decided on your GROUP COVENANT. This becomes your game plan.

**1.** The purpose of our group is . . .

**2.** Our specific goals are . . .

**3.** We will meet _____ times, every _____ week, after which we will evaluate our group.

**4.** We will meet: Day of week _____ from _____ (time) to _____ .

**5.** We will meet at _____ , or rotate the place where we meet.

**6.** In addition to the study of the Bible, we will . . .

**7.** We will adhere to the following ground rules:
- ☐ The leader of the group will be . . . or we will rotate the leadership.
- ☐ The host for each meeting (other than the leader) will be . . . or we will rotate this responsibility.
- ☐ Food/refreshments will be . . .
- ☐ Baby-sitting, etc.

**8.** In addition to these general rules, we will agree to the following disciplines:
- ☐ Attendance: To give priority to the group meetings
- ☐ Participation: To share responsibility for the group
- ☐ Confidentiality: To keep anything that is said strictly confidential
- ☐ Accountability: To give permission to group members to hold you accountable for goals you set for yourself
- ☐ Accessibility: To give one another the right to call upon you for help in time of need—even in the middle of the night.

ARE YOU FEELING A LITTLE

# DISTANT FROM THE OTHERS IN YOUR GROUP?

**SYMPTOMS:** Does your group start off like a Model A Ford on a cold morning? Or sag in the middle when you get to the Bible study? Do you find some of the people do all the talking . . . and others never get out of their "shell"?

**PRESCRIPTION:** Use the "flow questions" in the margin, next to the Scripture text, to guide the discussion. The questions are carefully designed to explode like time bombs on three levels of sharing: (1) TO BEGIN—to break the ice, (2) READ SCRIPTURE AND DISCUSS—to discuss the Scripture text, and (3) TO CLOSE AND PRAY—to take inventory of your own life.

**1** **TO BEGIN / 10–15 Minutes:** Start off with a few good "stories" about your childhood or human-interest experiences. The better the "stories" at this level . . . the deeper the group will share at the close. (There is a close parallel between "childlikeness" and "Christlikeness".)

**TO BEGIN / 15 Minutes** (Choose 1 or 2)

❏ What mail will you open first: Bills? Official looking stuff? Personal mail? Love letter?
❏ When you care for someone, are you more likely to send a funny card or a touching one?

**2** **READ SCRIPTURE AND DISCUSS / 30–45 Minutes:** You read the Scripture text at this point and go around on the first question. The questions are designed both to get you into the text and to help you reflect on the Scripture's meaning for your own life. The questions will help to draw your group together in a way that all can participate and share. By the way, you do not have to finish all the questions. Save time for the TO CLOSE AND PRAY section.

**READ SCRIPTURE AND DISCUSS / 30 Minutes**

❏ Where is Paul writing from? Why? Who is he writing to? (Hint: Go back and read the Introduction, especially the paragraph on Origin and Occasion.)
❏ Who was the Apostle Paul in your spiritual life—who introduced you to Jesus Christ and cared about your spiritual growth?

**3** **TO CLOSE AND PRAY / 15–30 Minutes** This is the heart of the Bible study. The purpose is to take inventory of your own life and share with the group "what God is telling you to do." The questions are "high risk"; that is, the group is asked to share on a "need level," before moving on to prayer.

**TO CLOSE AND PRAY / 15-30 Minutes**

❏ If you had a spiritual check-up today, what would the doctor prescribe?
❏ How can this Bible study group help you reach your spiritual goals?
❏ Who is someone you would like to invite to this group next week?
❏ What would you like this group to remember in prayer for you this week?

## Scripture

Thanksgiving and Prayer

*³I thank my God every time I remember you. ⁴In all my prayers for all of you, I always pray with joy ⁵because of your partnership in the gospel from the first day until now, ⁶being confident of this, that he who began a good work in you will carry it on to completion until the day of Christ Jesus.*
*⁷It is right for me to feel this way about all of you, since I have you in my heart;*

## Group Questions

**TO BEGIN:** What mail will you open first:Bills? Official looking stuff? Personal mail? Love letter?

**READ SCRIPTURE AND DISCUSS:** Where is Paul writing from? Why? Who is he writing to? (Hint: Go back and read the Introduction, especially the paragraph on Origin and Occasion).

**TO CLOSE AND PRAY:** If you had a spiritual check-up today, what would the doctor pre-scribe?

# ARE YOU FEELING A LITTLE
# INTIMIDATED BY THE BIBLE SCHOLARS IN YOUR GROUP?

**SYMPTOMS:** Are you afraid that your ignorance about the Bible could be embarrassing? For instance: if someone asked you who Melchizedek was, what would you say? If you said "an old linebacker for the Raiders", you would be wrong. Twice wrong.

**PRESCRIPTION:** Don't despair. Most of the people in your group don't know either. And that's O.K. This Bible study group is for BEGINNERS. And for BEGINNERS, there are Notes on the opposite page to help you keep up to speed with the rest of the group.

NOTES include:

☐ Definitions of significant words.

☐ Historical background: the political, social, economic context behind the words in the text.

☐ Geographical setting: facts about the country, terrain, lakes, crops, roads, and religious shrines.

☐ Cultural perspective: lifestyles, homes, customs, holidays, traditions, and social patterns.

☐ Archeological evidence: recent findings that sheds light on the Bible events.

☐ Summary/Commentary: recap of the argument to keep the passage in the context of the whole book.

---

## Notes

**1:3 every time I remember you**. This is a difficult phrase to translate from the Greek. What it seems to mean is that during his times of prayer, Paul "was compelled by love to mention his Philippian friends. This means, then, that Paul gave thanks not whenever he happened to remember them, but that he regularly gave thanks for them and mentioned them to God at set times of prayer" (Hawthorne).

**1:4 with joy**. "Joy" is a theme that pervades Philippians. This is the first of some fourteen times that Paul will use the word in this epistle. He mentions "joy" more often in this short epistle

**confirming the gospel**. These are legal terms. The reference is to Paul's defense before the Roman court, in which he hopes to be able not only to vindicate himself and the gospel from false charges, but to proclaim the gospel in life-changing power to those in the courtroom. (See Ac 26 for an example of how Paul did this when he stood in court before Agrippa and Festus.)

**1:8 I long**. Yet another word characteristic of Paul. He uses it seven of the nine times it is found in the New Testament. This is a strong word and expresses the depth of Paul's feelings for them, his desire to be with them, and the wish to minister

ARE YOU FEELING A LITTLE

# TEMPTED TO KEEP THE GROUP JUST FOR YOURSELF?

---

**SYMPTOMS:** Two feelings surface: (1) if we let anyone into our group, it would destroy our "closeness", and/or (2) if we let anyone into our group, we would not have time enough to share.

**PRESCRIPTION:** Study the ministry of Jesus and the early church: the need for "closeness" and the danger of "closedness." How did Jesus respond to his own disciples when they asked to "stay together" and build a "monument." Note the Story of the Transfiguration in Mark 9:2–13.

**SOLUTION #1:** Pull up an empty chair during the prayer time at the close of the group and pray that God will "fill the chair" with someone by the next week.

**SOLUTION #2:** When the group reaches seven or eight in number, divide into two groups of 4—4 at the dining table, 4 at the kitchen table—when the time comes for the Bible study . . . and reshuffle the foursomes every week so that you keep the whole group intact, but sub-group for the discussion time.

---

### THREE PART AGENDA FOR GROUP USING THE SUB-GROUP MODEL

**GATHERING/15 Minutes/All Together.**
Refreshments are served as the group gathers and assignments are made to sub-groups of 4.

**SHARING/30–45 Minutes/Groups of 4.**
Sub-groups are formed to discuss the questions in the margin of the text.

**CARING/15–30 Minutes/All Together.**
Regather the whole group to share prayer requests and pray.

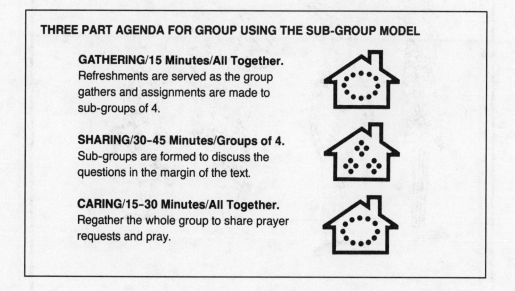

## ARE YOU FEELING A LITTLE

# BORED WITH YOUR BIBLE STUDY GROUP?

**SYMPTOMS:** You feel "tired" before the meeting starts. And worse after it is over. The sharing is mostly a "head-trip". One person is absent three weeks in a row. Another is chronically late. You feel like your time could be better spent doing something else, but you don't know how to say it.

**PRESCRIPTION:** You may be having a group "mid-life" crisis. Here are three suggestions.

1. Call "time out" for a session and evaluate your Covenant (page 5). Are you focused on your "purpose"? Your goals? Are you sticking to your rules? Should you throw out some of your rules? (Nobody said you can't.)

2. Check to see if your group is hitting on all three cylinders for a healthy small group. (1) Nurture/Bible Study, (2) Support for one another, and (3) Mission/Task. Here's a way to test yourself.
   On a scale from 1 to 10, circle a number to indicate how you feel your group is doing on each of these three cylinders.

   **ON NURTURE/BIBLE STUDY:** Getting to know the Bible. Letting God speak to you about His plans for your life through the Scripture.

   | We're doing a LOUSY JOB | 1 | 2 | 3 | 4 | 5 | 6 | 7 | 8 | 9 | 10 | We're doing a GREAT JOB |
   |---|---|---|---|---|---|---|---|---|---|---|---|

   **ON SUPPORT:** Getting to know each other. Caring about each other. Holding each other accountable for the best God has for you.

   | We're doing a LOUSY JOB | 1 | 2 | 3 | 4 | 5 | 6 | 7 | 8 | 9 | 10 | We're doing a GREAT JOB |
   |---|---|---|---|---|---|---|---|---|---|---|---|

   **ON MISSION/TASK:** Reaching out to others in need. Drawing people into the group, or sponsoring another group.

   | We're doing a LOUSY JOB | 1 | 2 | 3 | 4 | 5 | 6 | 7 | 8 | 9 | 10 | We're doing a GREAT JOB |
   |---|---|---|---|---|---|---|---|---|---|---|---|

3. Consider the possibility that God is saying it is time to shut down the group. Take time for a party. Give everyone a chance to share what the group has meant to him/her and what he/she will remember most about the group.

**ARE YOU FEELING A LITTLE**

# ITCHY ABOUT DOING SOMETHING MORE?

**SYMPTOMS:** You're feeling tired of just sitting around studying the Bible. You have friends who are really hurting. Struggling. God seems to be saying something, but you don't know just what.

**PRESCRIPTION:** Consider the possibility that God is asking your group to split up and give birth to some new groups. Here are some steps:

1. Brainstorm together. Go around and have everyone finish the first sentence below. Then, go around on the second sentence, etc.

   I am concerned about a group for . . . (such as . . . "a group for young mothers, single parents, blended families, parents of adolescents, men at my office, young couples, empty nesters . . ." etc.).

   I wish we could . . .

   I would be willing to . . .

2. Make a list of prospects (people from the fringe of the church or outside of any church) that you would like to invite to a dinner party at which you could explain "what this Bible study group has meant to you."

3. Write each of these people a hand-written invitation on your personal stationary, inviting them to the dinner party at your home. (Don't bother to use the church bulletin. Nobody reads that.)

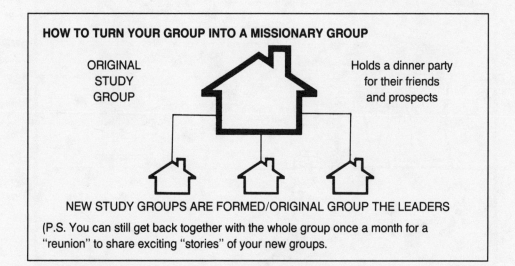

**HOW TO TURN YOUR GROUP INTO A MISSIONARY GROUP**

ORIGINAL STUDY GROUP

Holds a dinner party for their friends and prospects

NEW STUDY GROUPS ARE FORMED/ORIGINAL GROUP THE LEADERS

(P.S. You can still get back together with the whole group once a month for a "reunion" to share exciting "stories" of your new groups.

ply had an amazing story to tell by which God's nature would be revealed.

**1:20 *Decapolis.*** A league of 10 Gentile cities patterned after the Greek way of life. This is the first of several ventures by Jesus into Gentile areas, demonstrating what Mark later points out (Mk 13:10; 14:9), that the Gospel is to be preached to all nations. Apparently the efforts of the ex-demoniac to tell others about Jesus were successful. When Jesus returns to this region again he is greeted by enthusiastic crowds who know of his power to heal (Mark 7:31–37). Now Jesus must instruct them—as he has done all along with his Jewish audiences—not to tell anyone about his healing power (Mark 7:36). Furthermore, following the account of the healing of the deaf and dumb man in Mark 7:31–37, Mark tells the story of the feeding of the 4,000. Unlike the feeding of the 5,000 in which the crowd was made up of Jews, here there are Gentile's present. Why were they there? In this story about casting out the legion of demons the people are asking Jesus to leave. Now they gather around him. It may be that they had heard about Jesus from the witness of the ex-demoniac. Mark's Roman readers would find encouragement in the fact that right from the start the Lord ministered to non-Jews like themselves.

## Possession

This story provides a classic picture of demon possession. Trench describes it as "the sense of misery in which [the possessed] does not acquiesce, the deep feeling of inward discord, of the true life utterly shattered, of an alien power which has mastered him wholly, and now is truly lording over him, and ever drawing farther away from him in who only [people] can find rest and peace." The demoniacs here express the inner struggle: while defying Jesus, they yet run to him. This confusion, agony, misery, and "this yearning after deliverance, was, in fact, what made these demoniacs objects and subjects for Christ's healing power."

To be possessed is thus not the same as to be wicked. A wicked person can be quite at peace with his or her evil: A possessed person is in inner torment. In Shakespeare, a man like Iago is evil whereas a man like Hamlet is possessed.

Possession is also not a superstitious way of describing lunacy or mental illness. Even in ancient times, people recognized a difference between someone who was insane and someone possessed.

Possession by evil spirits is not unknown today. While the presence of the gospel has limited the activity of spirits in this way, the decline of Christian commitment in Western cultures is being greeted with an increasing awareness of cases of possession. It appears that occult activity, Satanic cults, mind-altering chemicals, and promiscuous sexual immorality are risk factors in providing a means of entry for spiritual possession, although sinful living by no means necessarily leads to possession.

The antidote to spiritual possession is clear from the gospel: Those who embrace Jesus Christ as Lord, who cultivate their relationship to him and seek to practice his teachings are protected from the attacks of the Evil One through the agency of God's Spirit. One major aspect of the gospel is that Jesus has freed people from the grasp of the devil. This story highlights the freedom and wholeness Jesus brings to those who trust him: They are free from demonic forces; they are restored and healed. All this comes, not through elaborate rituals of exorcism, and certainly not through acts of appeasement to Satan as are practiced in some Satanic cults, but through the word of deliverance pronounced by Jesus. All those who call upon the Lord shall be saved!

# UNIT 7—Water Into Wine / John 2:1–11

## Scripture

___

Jesus Changes Water to Wine

*2 On the third day a wedding took place at Cana in Galilee. Jesus' mother was there, ²and Jesus and his disciples had also been invited to the wedding. ³When the wine was gone, Jesus' mother said to him, "They have no more wine."*

*⁴"Dear woman, why do you involve me?" Jesus replied. "My time has not yet come."*

*⁵His mother said to the servants, "Do whatever he tells you."*

*⁶Nearby stood six stone water jars, the kind used by the Jews for ceremonial washing, each holding from twenty to thirty gallons.ᵃ*

*⁷Jesus said to the servants, "Fill the jars with water"; so they filled them to the brim.*

*⁸Then he told them, "Now draw some out and take it to the master of the banquet."*

*They did so, ⁹and the master of the banquet tasted the water that had been turned into wine. He did not realize where it had come from, though the servants who had drawn the water knew. Then he called the bridegroom aside ¹⁰and said, "Everyone brings out the choice wine first and then the cheaper wine after the guests have had too much to drink; but you have saved the best till now."*

*¹¹This, the first of his miraculous signs, Jesus performed at Cana in Galilee. He thus revealed his glory, and his disciples put their faith in him.*

ᵃ6 Greek *two to three metretes* (probably about 75 to 115 liters)

# Group Questions

**TO BEGIN / 15 Minutes** (Choose 1 or 2)

❏ What is the funniest thing that happened at a wedding you attended?
❏ What is the most enjoyable wedding reception you have been to?
❏ When is the last time your mother embarrassed you in public?

**READ SCRIPTURE AND DISCUSS / 30 Minutes**

❏ What do you remember about Jewish weddings from the movie *Fiddler On The Roof?*
❏ Given the importance of social customs (see Note for 2:3) what is going on in the kitchen behind the scenes?
❏ In the Notes, you find an interesting translation of Jesus' response to his mother (Mother, let me handle this). What is Jesus trying to avoid and why?
❏ Who were the only people in this story who knew that the substance in the jars was really water? What did the catering manager (the master of the banquet) think?
❏ What is meant by the word "sign" to describe this miracle?
❏ What is the "wine" level (zest for life) in your life at the moment? Full? Half full? Empty?
❏ What is draining you? What area of your life feels like stale water in an old jug?

**TO CLOSE AND PRAY / 15–30 Minutes**

❏ What is the most exciting thing in your spiritual life right now?
❏ What are you looking forward to next week?
❏ How can this group pray for you?

# Notes

**Summary.** In the next four units we will be examining a series of miracles that show Jesus' power over nature. The first few miracles have to do with food: turning water into wine (Unit 7) and multiplying a few loaves and fish into food enough to feed thousands (Unit 8). In Units 9 and 10 we examine two water miracles: Jesus calming a sea storm and Jesus walking on water. These so-called nature miracles move us into a new category of miracle. It is not difficult for most of us to believe that Jesus cured people; we have heard about (or seen) the same thing happen in our day and age. It is only one step beyond faith healing to the casting out of demons. Although we may be a little uncomfortable with the idea of demons possessing people, our commitment to the reality of the supernatural makes it possible for us to accept exorcism. Besides, one hears about demons being cast out even today. But when it comes to circumventing the so-called laws of nature, then we wonder. Not that Jesus could do it—he is God's son—but what it all means to us today.

This incident is the first of seven signs around which chapters 2–12 of John's Gospel are built. These miracles (2:11; 4:43–54; 5:1–11; 6:1–13, 16–21; 9:1–11; 11:38–44) are specifically called "signs" because they are not simply acts of power, but are meant to demonstrate the glory of God in Jesus (1:14). They are presented so that the reader might share in the confession that "these (signs) are written that you may believe that Jesus is the Son of God, and that by believing you may have life in his name" (20:31). In this story, the growing recognition of who Jesus is climaxes with the affirmation of the disciples' faith (2:11).

**2:1 *On the third day.*** It has been observed that John's Gospel is an extended meditation on the meaning of Jesus' death and resurrection, since from the very beginning of the Gospel there are allusions to these events (i.e., "the Lamb of God" in 1:29; Jesus' reference to the destruction of his body and the resurrection in 2:19; the reference to Jesus being lifted up in 3:14). The reference here to the "third day" begs us to read this story in light of the reality of Christ's resurrection on the third day after his death. This story highlights both the new quality of life brought into being through Jesus' death and resurrection, and his intention to replace the formal religious structures of his day with the reality of joyful intimacy with God.

# Notes (Continued)

**wedding.** Weddings were important social events; a time when all the relatives and townspeople would gather to celebrate, often for up to a week!

**Cana.** The exact location of this village is unknown but it is believed to have been near Nazareth.

**2:2 Jesus and his disciples.** According to John's chronology thus far, Jesus only has five disciples, all residents of the immediate area (1:35,40–41, 43–49).

**2:3 When the wine was gone.** This was potentially a very humiliating social situation. It would reflect badly on the host as someone too miserly to provide adequate refreshments for the guests.

**They have no more wine.** Why Jesus' mother approached Jesus with this concern is unknown, since Jesus had not previously done anything to make her expect he could solve the problem. It implies her awareness of his role as the divinely appointed ruler of Israel, and perhaps is an encouragement on her part to start acting the part!

**2:4 Dear woman.** Jesus uses this same term to address other women (Matt. 15:28; Luke 13:12). It is not a harsh term, but it is an unusual term for a son to use with his mother. "That Jesus calls Mary 'Woman' and not Mother' probably indicates that there is a new relationship between them as He enters on His public ministry" (Morris).

**why do you involve me?** Since the time for his Messianic role is at hand, Jesus is making it clear that from now on no other loyalties and relationships will be allowed to dominate that agenda. Barclay translates this as "Lady, let me handle this in my own way."

**My time has not yet come.** John frequently uses phrases and words with double meanings. Here, this phrase appears to mean simply that it is not yet appropriate for him to act. However, the "time" or "hour" of Jesus in this Gospel (7:6,8,30; 8:20; 12:23, 2; 13:1) has a theological meaning as well. It is used to refer to those moments when things happen "to and through Jesus which reveal his ... majesty and authority" (Brown) culminating in his crucifixion (16:32; 17:1). Jesus' response to Mary in this scene communicates that he will not operate on any other time frame nor for any other purpose than the one his

Father has assigned him.

**2:5 Do whatever he tells you.** Again (see v. 3), the reason for Mary's confidence in pressing on with this concern is unknown. The phrase does serve to show that the initiative is left with Jesus.

**2:6 six stone water jars.** Although not required by the law of Moses, by Jesus' day many Jews, in order to show their devotion to God, practiced purification rituals based on those required of the priests (Ex 30:19–20; Mark 7:1–4 ). For instance, water would be poured over the hands of the guests prior to the meal. A large event like this wedding would require a great deal of water for such cleansing. The fact that it is these jars that are used implies that the old ways of ritual purification are going to be radically transformed by Jesus.

**twenty to thirty gallons.** The drinking of wine did not have the associations with alcoholism and alcohol abuse as it does so often today. The use of wine was a way of showing hospitality to guests, an expression of one's desire that others join in as celebrants at a happy occasion. Jesus' provision of such an ample amount of wine puts him in the place of a host, generously and graciously providing for his guests. This story enacts the parable of the bridegroom and of the new wine found in Mark 2:19–20; 2:22. The new wine Jesus gives totally transforms the old water of a formalized religion into a relationship with God characterized by joy and abundance (see 1:16). Feasting and the abundance of wine is a characteristic image used in the OT to describe the joy of God's people who have experienced his deliverance (Isa 25:6; 55:1–2). This celebration is to begin because of the presence of Jesus.

**2:9 the master of the banquet.** This appears to have been an honored guest at the wedding, serving in a role somewhat akin to that of a modern–day toastmaster.

**He did not realize where it had come from.** This parallels the theme throughout John's Gospel that the identity of Jesus is revealed only to those he chooses. Others see but do not comprehend.

**He called the bridegroom.** Weddings were typically held at the home of the groom or of his parents. The groom would be responsible for planning the wedding.

# Notes (Continued)

**2:10** *Everyone brings out the choice wine first.* Typically, the best wine would be served when the guests would be most able to appreciate it. Later on, when they are less likely to notice, a cheaper quality of wine would be introduced. The quality of this wine was such that the master of the banquet thought the bridegroom had for some reason reversed the normal procedure.

**2:11** *miraculous signs.* Although the other Gospels typically refer to Jesus' miracles with a word that shows they are works of power, John prefers to call them signs. This encourages his readers to see these actions as pointers to God's presence in Jesus (John 1:12). Likewise, they are physical and material illustrations of the spiritual life Jesus came to bring.

*glory.* While the master of the banquet failed to consider by whom the wine came, the disciples saw the reality behind the sign. This was their first glimpse of the light of God's glory manifested in Jesus. The fact that this act involves creative power serves to indicate that "the Word became flesh" (1:14). His generous provision of such a great amount of wine and his ability to transform a potentially dismal situation into one of richness and abundance witnesses to the fact that "From the fullness of his grace we have all received one blessing after another" (1:16). The fact that it was the contents of the jars used for the rites of purification that were transformed indicates that in him a new era has dawned. The ritualistic forms of Jewish piety are to be replaced by Jesus with a relationship with God that is truly life-giving.

# Insights From the Commentators

This story would make sense to both the Jews and Greeks in John's audience. To the Jews, the story points out that Jesus has come to "transform the imperfection of the law into the perfection of grace" (Barclay). Jewish ritualism is to the nature of the spiritual life Jesus comes to bring like water is to wine at a wedding! At the same time, John's Greek readers might be reminded of a story from their mythology. The Greek god Dionysos was associated with the power to transform water into wine. In light of that background, "... to the Greeks John said, 'Jesus has come really and truly to do the things you only dreamed the gods could do' " (Barclay).

Colin Brown makes an important observation about the nature of Jesus' miracles as "signs": "(The miracles) are signs of God's kingly rule, the dawn of which Jesus announced in his proclamation ... the miracles are a foreshadowing and a promise of the coming universal redemption. Ultimately, it is in this eschatalogical context that the accounts of Jesus' miracles are to be read. Thus, the casting out of demons signals God's invasion into the realm of Satan and its final annihilation; the raising of the dead announces that death will be forever done away with; the healing of the sick bears witness to the cessation of all suffering; the miraculous provisions of food are foretokens of the end of all physical need; the stilling of the storm points forward to the complete victory over the powers of chaos which threaten the earth." *(New International Dictionary of New Testament Theology,* Vol. 2, p. 631, *Miracle)*

Karl Barth notes, "What took place were promises and ... anticipations of a ... kind of life in which there will be no more sorrow, tears, and crying, and where death as the last enemy will be no more." *(Evangelical Theology: An Introduction,* pp. 68–69)

# UNIT 8—Jesus Feeds the Five Thousand / Mark 6:30–44

## Scripture

Jesus Feeds the Five Thousand

*30The apostles gathered around Jesus and reported to him all they had done and taught. 31Then, because so many people were coming and going that they did not even have a chance to eat, he said to them, "Come with me by yourselves to a quiet place and get some rest."*

*32So they went away by themselves in a boat to a solitary place. 33But many who saw them leaving recognized them and ran on foot from all the towns and got there ahead of them. 34When Jesus landed and saw a large crowd, he had compassion on them, because they were like sheep without a shepherd. So he began teaching them many things.*

*35By this time it was late in the day, so his disciples came to him. "This is a remote place," they said, "and it's already very late. 36Send the people away so they can go to the surrounding countryside and villages and buy themselves something to eat."*

*37But he answered, "You give them something to eat."*

*They said to him, "That would take eight months of a man's wages!ª Are we to go and spend that much on bread and give it to them to eat?"*

*38"How many loaves do you have?" he asked. "Go and see." When they found out, they said, "Five—and two fish."*

*39Then Jesus directed them to have all the people sit down in groups on the green grass. 40So they sat down in groups of hundreds and fifties. 41Taking the five loaves and the two fish and looking up to heaven, he gave thanks and broke the loaves. Then he gave them to his disciples to set before the people. He also divided the two fish among them all. 42They all ate and were satisfied, 43and the disciples picked up twelve basketfuls of broken pieces of bread and fish. 44The number of the men who had eaten was five thousand.*

ª37 Greek *take two hundred denarii*

# Group Questions

**TO BEGIN / 15 Minutes** (Choose 1 or 2)

❏ When have you gone the longest without food? For what reason?
❏ If you had to feed 5,000 people at a big church gathering, what would you serve? How would you organize it?
❏ What do you do to unwind after a busy day?

**READ SCRIPTURE AND DISCUSS / 30 Minutes**

❏ The apostles have just returned from an exhausting preaching mission. Jesus decides to take them away for a little relaxation. If you had been one of the apostles, how would you be feeling?
❏ Surprise. When they arrive, 5,000 people are there to greet them. What is the difference between the way Jesus looked on the people and the way the disciples looked on them?
❏ How did the disciples respond when Jesus asked them to feed the crowd?
❏ What is the principle here in the way Jesus went about performing this miracle? If God can multiply food, why save the scraps?
❏ What is the closest you have come to feeling the stress and distress in trying to respond to overwhelming needs?
❏ Compassion fatigue is a recognized illness today among teachers, social workers, caregivers and church workers. Are you experiencing some of these symptoms?
❏ When do you feel most inadequate and short of resources as you look at the needs around you?
❏ If you knew you could not fail, what would be one thing you would like to do in the near future? What is keeping you from trying this?

**TO CLOSE AND PRAY / 15–30 Minutes**

❏ If God called you on the phone today and asked you to do something special for your community, what would you say?
❏ How can this group encourage and support you?
❏ What would you like this group to pray for you in the next week?

## Notes

**Summary.** The incident that we will study in this unit—the feeding of the 5,000—is special: It is the only miracle that is reported in all four Gospels. Its importance, therefore, is not to be overlooked. Mark uses this familiar story to begin another major section (Mark 6:30–8:30) in his Gospel. In the first section of the Gospel (Mark 1:14–4:34) the disciples (and others) view Jesus as an exceptionally gifted rabbi. In section two (Mark 4:35–6:29), Jesus is discovered to be a man of amazing power. Here in section three, he is discovered to be the Messiah (Mark 8:27–30). Thus the disciples' understanding of Jesus continues to unfold. In this section there are two parallel cycles of stories. The point is made in both cycles that it will take a miracle from Jesus to heal the hardened hearts of the Twelve so that they come to see who he really is—or at least to understand as much as they can prior to his death and resurrection. Cycle one (Mark 6:30–7:37) begins with the feeding of the 5,000 and ends with the healing of a deaf and dumb man. Cycle two (Mark 8:1–26) begins with the feeding of the 4,000 and ends with the healing of a blind man. In both cycles the reader is shown the inability of the disciples to understand what is happening. It is as if they are deaf, dumb and blind, in need of healing if they are to understand who Jesus is.

In this story, Mark begins to reveal who Jesus really is. Mark does not do this directly. He does it symbolically. The fact that there are two feeding stories in Mark points in this direction. One feeding story is all that would have been necessary if the point Mark wants to make is that Jesus can perform such a miracle. Furthermore, the two stories differ in the symbols they contain. The feeding of the 5,000 is filled with symbols that point to Jesus' role in Israel. The feeding of the 4,000 is filled with symbols that point to his role with the Gentiles.

Here in the feeding of the 5,000 the symbols allude to Moses and David. Jesus is seen to be the new Moses and the new David. Thus he is revealed to be the long expected, now returning King of Israel, the Messiah. That the disciples come to understand the meaning of these symbolic elements is demonstrated by Peter's declaration in Mark 8:29 (at the end of this unit) that they know that Jesus is the Messiah. No other information has been presented to the Twelve that would lead them to this conclusion apart from seeing Jesus function as the new Moses and new David in the two feeding stories.

# Notes (Continued)

**6:30** Having returned from their mission to preach, cast out demons, and heal in the villages throughout Galilee (Mark 5:7–12), the Twelve report to the Lord what took place in their travels.

**apostles.** This is the only time this term is used in Mark. Here it is not so much a title as a description of what they have just done. An apostle is "one who is sent" and they have just completed the missionary work the Lord sent them out to do (v. 7).

**6:31 get some rest.** It is Jesus who insists on rest even though the opportunity for ministry is great (see also 1:35).

**6:33 ran on foot.** The crowds are now wise to the disciples' tactic of simply sailing off across the lake and leaving them standing on the shore (see Mark 4:35–36). So they follow on foot. The distances would not have been great since the lake was only eight miles at its widest. As they run around the lake to get to the place where the boats would land, more and more people from the lakeside villages would join with them, swelling their numbers.

**6:34 sheep without a shepherd.** Without a shepherd, sheep are hopelessly lost. They have no way to defend themselves and they will probably starve. This was an apt metaphor for the condition of the crowd. They had been abandoned, by and large, by the religious leaders. Their inability to keep the oral law caused them to be considered "unclean" in a religious sense. This phrase seems to be an allusion to Numbers 27:15–17 in which Moses describes the kind of person needed to lead Israel after he is gone: "Moses said to the LORD, 'May the LORD, the God of the spirits of all mankind, appoint a man over this community to go out and come in before them, one who will lead them out and bring them in, so the LORD's people will not be like sheep without a shepherd." Furthermore, this phrase recalls Ezekiel 34 in which God promises to feed his "sheep" by sending a king like David to be their shepherd: "I will place over them one shepherd, my servant David, and he will tend them; he will tend them and be their shepherd" (Ezekiel 34:23). This is the first of several allusions that connect Jesus with Moses and David. Jesus is the ultimate fulfillment of Moses' prayer and Ezekiel's prophetic words. This is the first of several allusions to Moses and David and to the fact that Jesus fulfills their roles with Israel.

**6:35** The disciples recognize that they have a problem on their hands. How are they going to feed the enormous crowd that has gathered?

**a remote place.** For the third time Mark makes the point that all this takes place in a wilderness area (see vv. 31,32) reinforcing the connection to Moses who fed the people in the wilderness. Jesus himself, makes this very connection in John 6:26–51.

**6:36 Send the people away.** This is the disciples' solution! "Let the people buy what they need in the nearby towns." This is not a reasonable suggestion if the situation is viewed in ordinary terms for there are too many people for the supplies available in the local villages.

**6:37 "You give them something to eat."** Jesus has quite a different solution in mind! The response of the disciples indicates they had no clue as to how Jesus expected them to do this. Jesus statement, and the entire scene, is similar to that found in 2 Kings 4:42–44. In that situation Elisha, a great prophet of the Lord, miraculously provided food for 100 people from 20 loaves of bread. Once again, Jesus is connected to an Old Testament hero through whom God worked.

**eight months of a man's wages.** Once again, as during the storm on the lake (Mark 4:37–38), the disciples do not expect that Jesus will be able to solve the problem in a miraculous way. The only way they can see to feed the crowd is to buy lots of food, and they do not feel an expenditure that large is warranted.

**Are we to go and spend.** While this may mean that they did have enough money in their common purse to do this but were reluctant to spend it this way, it is more likely that this was a rhetorical question tinged with sarcasm. Elsewhere in this Gospel, the disciples express frustration at what seems to be an unreasonable suggestion or question by Jesus (see Mark 4:30–31,38). Their exasperation with Jesus is evident in their two responses to him in this verse.

**6:39 groups on the green grass.** A lovely, descriptive touch which could only come from an eye witness. The people sat in groups in their bright red and yellow robes on the green grass looking all the world like a flower garden spread out across the hills. (The word translated "groups" was used to describe a

# Notes (Continued)

Greek garden.) It was mid-April since it was only then that the grass was green. This descriptive touch is loaded with implications. Mark does not typically use descriptive adjectives (i.e., "green") in his writing. The fact that he does so here suggests an allusion to Psalm 23:2, a psalm of David in which God, the shepherd of God's people, leads his flock to "lie down in green pastures." As with verse 34 (see Note), Mark is giving another verbal clue to the reader of the Messianic nature of Jesus.

**6:40 *groups of hundreds and fifties.*** During the wilderness march, Moses organized the people into similar groups (Ex 18:21).

**6:41 *five loaves.*** These were small round cakes made of wheat or barley. In keeping with the metaphoric nature of this story, the five loaves remind the readers of the teaching of Moses in the first five books of the OT. This strengthens the connection between Jesus and Moses. Furthermore, what Jesus does here is what Moses did in the wilderness: he feeds the hungry multitudes (compare Exo. 16, Num. 11).

***two fish.*** These were probably smoked or pickled fish that were used as a sauce for the bread.

***gave thanks.*** A common Jewish blessing at meals was "Blessed art thou, O Lord our God, king of the universe, who bringest forth bread from the earth" (Mann).

***gave thanks / broke / gave.*** Clearly Mark intends his readers to recall the Eucharist in this story. The words that he uses parallel the works of institution taken from the description of the Last Supper (which are later given in Mark 14:22): "Jesus took bread, gave thanks, and broke it ..." These are the words that Paul uses when he discusses the Eucharist: "The Lord Jesus, on the night he was betrayed, took bread, and when he had given thanks, he broke it and said, 'This is my body, which is for you; do this in remembrance of me.' " (1 Cor 11:23–24). This feeding, like the Eucharist, is a foreshadowing of the feeding of all God's people at the Messianic banquet.

**6:42 *satisfied.*** Miraculously, the five loaves and two fish fed everyone not meagerly but abundantly so that they were filled. As in the scene with Elisha (2 Ki 4:44), there was more than enough to go around accenting God's lavish generosity.

**6:43 *twelve.*** In keeping with the metaphoric nature of this story, the 12 baskets represent the 12 tribes of Israel. (In contrast, in the feeding of the 4,000 there are seven baskets; the number seven being connected with Gentiles.)

***basketfuls.*** These were small wicker containers carried by all Jews. Each disciple returned with his full. The word used for basket describes a distinctly Jewish type of basket. (In contrast, the word used for basket in the feeding of the 4000 refers to the ordinary Gentile basket.)

***broken pieces.*** The law required that scraps of a meal be collected.

**6:44 *men.*** Literally, this is "males." Matthew 14:21 makes it clear there were women and children present as well. The actual number of people fed far exceeded 5,000.

# UNIT 9—Jesus Calms the Storm / Mark 4:35–41

## Scripture

Jesus Calms the Storm

*[35]That day when evening came, he said to his disciples, "Let us go over to the other side." [36]Leaving the crowd behind, they took him along, just as he was, in the boat. There were also other boats with him. [37]A furious squall came up, and the waves broke over the boat, so that it was nearly swamped. [38]Jesus was in the stern, sleeping on a cushion. The disciples woke him and said to him, "Teacher, don't you care if we drown?"*

*[39]He got up, rebuked the wind and said to the waves, "Quiet! Be still!" Then the wind died down and it was completely calm.*

*[40]He said to his disciples, "Why are you so afraid? Do you still have no faith?"*

*[41]They were terrified and asked each other, "Who is this? Even the wind and the waves obey him!"*

# Group Questions

## TO BEGIN / 15 Minutes (Choose 1 or 2)

❏ When you were growing up, where did you go or hide when a big storm came up?
❏ What is the closest you have come to losing your life in a storm?
❏ Who in your family is good at keeping calm in the storms of life?

## READ SCRIPTURE AND DISCUSS / 30 Minutes

❏ Why do you think Jesus suggested that they take this boat trip across the lake?
❏ If you had been one of the disciples in the boat when it was about to sink, what would you have done?
❏ Why do you think the disciples awakened Jesus?
❏ What was the tone in Jesus' voice when he said, "Why are you frightened?" Was he angry? Disappointed? Upset? Or just inquisitive?
❏ In this miracle, what did Jesus show he had the power over?
❏ What is the difference in the fear of the disciples in the storm and the fear at the end of the story?
❏ If you could compare your own life to the storm in the Scripture, where are you right now: Smooth sailing? Sensing a storm brewing? In the middle of the storm, bailing water? Cleaning up after the storm?
❏ "Quiet! Be Still!" If Jesus were to speak these words to you today, what would they mean ... in your own words?

## TO CLOSE AND PRAY / 15–30 Minutes

❏ As you grow in your spiritual faith, are you seeing any improvement in the way you handle storms in your life?
❏ How do you feel about sharing your personal needs with this group?
❏ How can this group help you this week in prayer?

# Notes

**Summary.** We now come to a new category of nature miracle: Jesus tames the elements. Up to this point the nature miracles have been focused within a small space: jugs of water turned into wine, bread multiplied so all can eat. But here Jesus tackles a vicious storm that had spread across a whole lake. Even in the twentieth century we know the power of nature to be untamable. We may now be able to predict and track hurricanes; we still can do nothing about them. We may understand the physics of volcanoes; we still cannot stop them. Furthermore, such natural phenomena pack energies far beyond anything human beings can produce. Hurricanes, typhoons, earthquakes, and volcanoes are all explosions of power far in excess of even our mightiest bombs.

This story begins a new section in Mark's Gospel. Prior to this passage, both Jesus' enemies and friends regarded Jesus as a rabbi. To be sure, he was not a typical rabbi in that the content and form of his teaching (e.g., Mark 1:27) and his profound ability to heal (e.g., Mark 1:34) and perform exorcisms (e.g., Mark 1:39) differed greatly from the norm. Nonetheless, both friend and foe assumed they understood basically who he was: a great teacher. However accomplished he was at his work, it still fit into what they knew a rabbi would do. This story is the first of four miracle stories which explode that category. Through these four stories, a whole new side of Jesus is revealed. While the earlier miracles in Mark dealt with healings and exorcisms, which, while certainly notable, were not without parallel among other rabbis, now he demonstrates his authority over the forces of nature and death. These four stories unveil the unique, awesome power of Jesus. The disciples see that he has authority over the very elements (Mark 4:35–41); over the most extreme case of possession by evil (Mark 5:1–20); over long-term, seemingly incurable disease (Mark 4:24–34); and even over death itself (Mark 4:21–24,36–43). No rabbi had this kind of power. At the end of the unit they discover that Jesus is not just a great teacher but a prophet. This is the new title that best explains what they have just witnessed. In fact, Jesus uses this title for himself for the first time in Mark's Gospel (Mark 6:4; see also 6:14–15). (See the Summary section in Unit 3, p. 19, for more details about the structure of Mark 4:35–5:43.)

**4:35 *That day.*** This story comes at the conclusion of a day of teaching by the lake (see Mark 4:1 where this day starts). Jesus is teaching in a boat that is anchored just off-shore. This was necessary due to the growing crowds and the people who were "pushing forward to touch him" (Mark 3:9–10). Such behavior was understandable. Who wouldn't want to touch Jesus or ask Jesus to heal in a day when there were no hospitals or reliable medicine? Being out on the lake also provided natural amplication for Jesus. When it is time to leave, Jesus does so by simply staying in the boat and sailing across the lake.

*when evening came.* This voyage begins as the sun is setting.

**4:36 *There were also other boats with him.*** Although these boats do not play any other role in the story, their mention, as well as that of other details not found in the parallel accounts (Matt. 8:23–27; Luke 8:22–25), indicate an eyewitness testimony of the event. Presumably the people in these boats were also saved when Jesus stilled the storm.

**4:37 *A furious squall.*** The Sea of Galilee was a deep, fresh-water lake, 13 miles long and eight miles wide at it widest point. It was pear-shaped and ringed by mountains, though open at its north and south ends. Fierce winds blew into this bowl-shaped sea creating savage and unpredictable storms.

*waves broke over the boat, so that it was nearly swamped.* In this succinct phrase Mark identifies the problem. The boat was filling with water. This reduced its maneuverability and, eventually would sink it. Bailing the water out of the boat was, therefore, of utmost importance.

**4:38 *sleeping.*** In the OT sleeping peacefully is a sign of trust in the power of God (e.g. Ps 4:8). The fact that Jesus was asleep during a storm is also a sign of his exhaustion from a day of teaching. Jesus slept in the back of the boat on the seat normally used by the helmsman.

*Teacher.* Up to this point, the disciples understood Jesus to be a rabbi.

*don't you care if we drown?* The disciples are scared. The storm threatens to swamp the boat. They need all the help they can get to bail out the water, but Jesus sleeps through it all. So they rouse him with this rather rude assertion. (Mark's Gospel does not glamorize the Twelve. See also Mark 5:31; 6:37; 8:4). As their later response indicates (v. 41),

they had no expectation that he would have any power over the storm.

**4:39** Instead of bailing, Jesus commands the wind and the waves to be still … and they obey. Thus, he demonstrates his power over the very elements in the same way that God does (see Ps 65:7; 106:9). This was something no ordinary rabbi could do.

*Be still!* This is literally, "Be muzzled!" as if the storm were some wild beast needing to be subdued. The same word was used to cast out the demon in the story in Mark 1:25. This command to silence presses God's peace into the strife that fights against God and his ways.

*completely calm.* This was a genuine miracle. When Jesus spoke it was not a matter of the wind beginning to slacken and the waves starting to die down. At one moment the Sea of Galilee was beset by a raging storm; at the next the lake was smooth and placid. What Jesus has done here reflects God's power and authority over the sea (see Ps 65:7; 89:9; 106:9; 107:23–32). Perhaps the most vivid example of God's power over the sea was his opening of the Red Sea so that Israel could pass through.

**4:40 *afraid.*** Some of the disciples were fishermen who knew how serious their peril was in the face of the storm. Because of the danger, actual fear for their lives was not inappropriate! However, once Jesus displays his power, their fear of the storm turns into fear of Jesus. This is the fear of the unknown and the unexplainable. The disciples were totally unprepared for his action.

*Do you still have no faith?* Faith here is "faith in God's helping power present and active in Jesus" (Cranfield). Although Jesus had not yet performed any miracle of this nature, the disciples "should by this time have learned something of the secret of the kingdom of God, which is the secret that the kingdom is come in the person and work of Jesus" (Cranfield). This miracle would force the disciples to reconsider all they had heard and seen from Jesus: What had he said or done that should lead them to expect he could act like this?

**4:41 *terrified.*** Terror replaced fear. This is what is felt in the presence of an unknown force or power. It is the response a vision of a demon, angel, ghost or some other strange, supernatural experience would inspire.

# Notes (Continued)

***Who is this?*** This is the key question with which Mark wrestles in his Gospel. The congregation in the synagogue where Jesus did his first miracle in Mark wondered about this (1:27). The religious leaders asked this question (2:7; 3:22). Now his disciples discover that even they do not understand who he is. Only the readers of the Gospel (1:1), God (1:11) and the demons (1:24,35) know his true identity. The rest of Mark describes how the disciples, in particular, overcome their culturally conditioned assumptions about who Jesus is and, step-by-step, discover his true nature. "In addition to the miracle's significance as a pointer to the secret of Jesus' person, Mark probably saw in it, and meant his readers to see, a symbolic significance. The parallel between the situation of the disciples on the lake and that of the Church in the midst of persecution would naturally suggest itself. (Very early a ship was a symbol of the Church in Christian art.) In the midst of persecution and all manners of perils, if Jesus be truly with his Church, then, even though his help may not at once be felt, his own must never doubt him, and need have no fear" (Cranfield, *St. Mark,* p. 175).

## Miracles or Superstition?
by C. S. Lewis

The nature miracles are sometimes explained away as the superstitious beliefs of pre-scientific people who were unaware of the laws of nature. As a critique of this assumption, C.S. Lewis comments:

"If the miracles were offered us as events that normally occurred, then the progress of science, whose business is to tell us what normally occurs, would render belief in them gradually harder and finally impossible. The progress of science has in just this way … made all sorts of things incredible which our ancestors believed: man-eating ants and gryphons in Scythia, men with one single gigantic foot, magnetic islands that drew all ships towards them, mermaids and fire-breathing dragons. But those things were never put forward as supernatural interruptions of the course of nature. They were put forward as items within her ordinary course—in fact as 'science.' Later and better science has therefore rightly removed them. Miracles are in a wholly different position … no one ever pretended that the Virgin Birth or Christ's walking on the water could be reckoned on to recur. When a thing professes from the very outset to be a unique invasion of Nature by something from outside, increasing knowledge of Nature can never make it more or less credible than it was at the beginning …The grounds for belief and disbelief are the same today as they were two thousand years ago. If Joseph had lacked faith to trust God or humility to perceive the holiness of his spouse, he could have disbelieved in the miraculous origin of her Son as easily as any modern man …" (*Miracles*, p. 49).

# UNIT 10—Jesus Walks on the Water / Matt. 14:22–36

## Scripture

Jesus Walks on the Water

*22Immediately Jesus made the disciples get into the boat and go on ahead of him to the other side, while he dismissed the crowd. 23After he had dismissed them, he went up on a mountainside by himself to pray. When evening came, he was there alone, 24but the boat was already a considerable distance*a *from land, buffeted by the waves because the wind was against it.*

*25During the fourth watch of the night Jesus went out to them, walking on the lake. 26When the disciples saw him walking on the lake, they were terrified. "It's a ghost," they said, and cried out in fear.*

*27But Jesus immediately said to them: "Take courage! It is I. Don't be afraid."*

*28"Lord, if it's you," Peter replied, "tell me to come to you on the water."*

*29"Come," he said.*

*Then Peter got down out of the boat, walked on the water and came toward Jesus. 30But when he saw the wind, he was afraid and, beginning to sink, cried out, "Lord, save me!"*

*31Immediately Jesus reached out his hand and caught him. "You of little faith," he said, "why did you doubt?"*

*32And when they climbed into the boat, the wind died down. 33Then those who were in the boat worshiped him, saying, "Truly you are the Son of God."*

*34When they had crossed over, they landed at Gennesaret. 35And when the men of that place recognized Jesus, they sent word to all the surrounding country. People brought all their sick to him 36and begged him to let the sick just touch the edge of his cloak, and all who touched him were healed.*

a24 Greek *many stadia*

# Group Questions

## Notes

**Summary.** Matthew, Mark and John all follow the story of the feeding of the 5,000 with this scene (Luke omits it). The two accounts differ in some details (Mark omits the scene of Peter attempting to walk on the water) and in their emphasis. In Matthew's account there are several miracles reported, not just one. First, the story we are examining comes immediately on the heels of the amazing miracle in which Jesus fed 5,000 people with a few loaves and some fish. Second, there is the miracle of Jesus walking on water (Matt 14:25). Third, there is the miracle of Peter walking on water—which, if anything, is even more amazing. We have already seen Jesus' power over nature so his walking on water, while extraordinary, fits in with what we have come to expect about him. But to extend this ability to another person is truly awesome (Matt 14:29). Finally, there is the miracle of healing in which it is only necessary to touch the hem of Jesus' garment (Matt 14:35–36).

### TO BEGIN / 15 Minutes (Choose 1 or 2)

- ❑ When you were growing up, who was the dare-devil among your friends?
- ❑ What is one of the craziest things you have ever done (or tried to do)?
- ❑ Of all of your boating experiences, which one is the most memorable?

### READ SCRIPTURE AND DISCUSS / 30 Minutes

- ❑ What do you remember about the story of the feeding of the 5,000 that occurred immediately before this story? Why do you think Jesus decided to dismiss the crowd and get out of there (see Note for 14:22)?
- ❑ If you had been one of the disciples in the boat when they saw someone walking on the water, what would you be thinking?
- ❑ What do you admire about Peter in this story? How does Peter remind you of yourself?
- ❑ How is this miracle different from the calming of the storm in the last study? How hard is it for you to believe that Jesus walked on water?
- ❑ When it comes to taking risks, how would you describe yourself?
- ❑ Where is God inviting you to step out of your comfortable boat and walk on the water with him?

### TO CLOSE AND PRAY / 15–30 Minutes

- ❑ What do you appreciate most about this group?
- ❑ What is your group planning to do after you finish this course?
- ❑ How can this group help you in prayer this week?

**14:22 *he dismissed the crowds.*** While neither Matthew nor Mark accounts for the abrupt departure of Jesus from the crowd, the reason is given in John 6:14–15. Apparently the crowd, sensing that the feeding of the 5,000 was a sign that Jesus was indeed the Messianic King for whom they had long been waiting, tried in its enthusiasm to make Jesus their king who would lead them in opposition to Rome. The disciples are sent away, perhaps, to keep them from harm in the face of this zealous crowd or perhaps to keep them from catching this false Messianic fever.

**14:23 *he went ... to pray.*** In the midst of great success and popular acclaim, once again Jesus goes off to pray. He is quick to acknowledge his dependence on God as the source of his power.

**14:24 *the wind was against it.*** Once again, the elements work against the disciples. (see Unit 9 for this account). This time the problem is not a storm, but a strong headwind that would make rowing very difficult.

**14:25 *the fourth watch.*** This was the way Roman soldiers marked time. The fourth watch ran from 3:00 to 6:00 a.m. Assuming the disciples set out to sea in the late afternoon, they had been struggling at the oars for probably seven or more hours.

# Notes (Continued)

***walking on the lake.*** While it has already been established that Jesus is Lord over the wind and the water (Mark 4:39,41), this is another new action that was well beyond the expectation of the disciples.

**14:26** ***terrified.*** Once again they are terrified by an event they did not expect and did not understand (see Mark 4:41). This is the terror of experiencing something that defies all categories of understanding.

***a ghost.*** The sea, especially at night, was thought to be a dwelling place for demons. The disciples had no idea what horror might await them as this apparition approached.

**14:27** ***"Take courage! It is I. Don't be afraid."*** This is the language of God. This call to have courage because of God's presence with his people is a common theme in the OT prophets (Isa 41:10; 43:5; Jer 1:8).

***"It is I."*** Literally, "I Am." This phrase can be understood to be a simple declaration by Jesus that there is no ghost to be afraid of. However, in the OT this is a phrase used by God to describe himself. (See esp. Exo. 3:1–14 where God reveals himself by this name to Moses in the burning bush.) This is the same phrase used by Jesus in his debate with the Jews by which he claims deity (see John 8:58). In the context of Jesus on-going self-revelation of himself to the disciples, this is a telling phrase. Jesus is not just a new Moses or another King in the line of David. He is also the Son of God. Since the OT often refers to God as the one who treads on the water (see Job 9:8; 38:16; Ps 77:19; Isa 43:2, 16), it is clear that his walking on the water was not simply another miracle: like the feeding of the 5,000, this was intended to be a sign of his divine identity. "Here is revelation of the Old Testament God in the person of Jesus ... The sea in the Old Testament stands for the uncanny power of chaos and death which threatens God's kingly rule. The theological point in this story is that in Jesus, God is asserting his sovereignty over the uncanny realm of Satan ... in the last resort (it) echoes the proclamation of Jesus: 'The Reign of God has drawn nigh' " (Fuller).

**14:28–32** This scene is found only in Matthew. "The scene of Peter walking (on) the sea contains something entirely unique: It shows the greatness of the promise made to faith within discipleship (14:28,29), but does not remain silent about the inability of the disciple to hold firmly to this promise during a time of testing (v. 30) ... It is probable that Peter is taken as a representative of the disciples (both those with Jesus and those in the church to whom Matthew was writing) in his enthusiastic love and insufficient faith" (Hill).

**14:28** ***if it's you.*** "If" should be understood in terms of "since." It is because Peter is sure that it is Jesus on the water that he asks permission to join him. He realizes he can only do so on the basis of Jesus' word and authority. Peter's action demonstrates what faith is all about: It is acting with confidence in Jesus even when circumstances seem to be impossible. It is not a foolhardiness based on personal bravado, but trust in the character of Jesus to protect and guide his people.

**14:30** At first it appears Peter was successful in this incredible act. However, the frightening uncertainty of the situation coupled with the power of the wind and waves beating against him led him to doubt Jesus' word: thus, he faltered.

***Lord, save me!*** Peter's cry sums up the cry of all those who find themselves in desperate situations: His hope is solely in Jesus to rescue him from the danger of the sea. Likewise, all disciples are to call upon Jesus to rescue them from the danger of sin. Matthew's story would encourage those in the church who likewise found themselves faltering along the path of discipleship when faced with threats to their safety. Faltering did not in itself disqualify one from Christ's care: instead, it can become a time to reach out afresh to him as Peter did.

**14:31** ***You of little faith.*** The problem Peter faced was not the circumstances, but inadequate trust in Jesus despite the circumstances. He has not yet fully come to trust in the power and the person of Jesus.

***the wind died down.*** This is not presented as a miracle in the same way as the calming of the winds in Mark 4:39 where Mark makes the point that the sea suddenly became "completely calm." However, Jesus probably had something to do with the slackening of the winds. He has been shown to have that kind of power and it is striking that they start to die down when he and Peter get into the boat.

# Notes (Continued)

**14:32 *Truly you are the Son of God.*** In fact, the disciples do not actually grasp who Jesus is until Caesarea Philippi (Matt 16:16). Their cry here, in the face of the dual miracle of Jesus and Peter walking on water, "represents more the instinctive reaction to a display of supernatural power. As the disciples groped for adequate words to express their awareness that Jesus was more than an ordinary man, this phrase came to mind, perhaps because of its Messianic connotations. The disciples' reaction here does not upstage Peter's deliberately Christological use of the title in 16:16, but prepares the way for it" (R.T. France).

***the Son of God.*** In the Old Testament, this term was used to describe God's appointed king who was to reign over Israel in God's stead (i.e., Ps 2:7). In the New Testament, the title is often used in connection with the title "Messiah." This scene highlights Jesus' divine appointment as God's representative and king since he exhibits the very power and authority of God.

**14:34 *Gennesaret.*** The wind having frustrated their plan to go north, they instead cross the lake to a thickly populated, fertile plain some four miles southwest of Capernaum

**14:36 *the edge of his cloak.*** This recalls the healing of the woman in Mark 5:25–28. The hem of a rabbi's garment was decorated with tassels representing the commands of God. There were probably some quasi-magical notions among the people that blended religious faith with superstitious practices so that it was assumed that these tassels possessed particularly effective powers. Or the point may be that Jesus was so powerful that even touching the very edge of his garment, i.e., making the most minimal contact with him, was sufficient to experience that power. Jesus was, indeed, a mighty healer in whom the power of God was at work.

# UNIT 11—Lazarus / John 11:1–3, 17–27, 38–47

## Scripture

**11** Now a man named Lazarus was sick. He was from Bethany, the village of Mary and her sister Martha. ²This Mary, whose brother Lazarus now lay sick, was the same one who poured perfume on the Lord and wiped his feet with her hair. ³So the sisters sent word to Jesus, "Lord, the one you love is sick."

### Jesus Comforts the Sisters

¹⁷On his arrival, Jesus found that Lazarus had already been in the tomb for four days. ¹⁸Bethany was less than two miles[a] from Jerusalem, ¹⁹and many Jews had come to Martha and Mary to comfort them in the loss of their brother. ²⁰When Martha heard that Jesus was coming, she went out to meet him, but Mary stayed at home.

²¹"Lord," Martha said to Jesus, "if you had been here, my brother would not have died. ²²But I know that even now God will give you whatever you ask."

²³Jesus said to her, "Your brother will rise again."

²⁴Martha answered, "I know he will rise again in the resurrection at the last day."

²⁵Jesus said to her, "I am the resurrection and the life. He who believes in me will live, even though he dies; ²⁶and whoever lives and believes in me will never die. Do you believe this?"

²⁷"Yes, Lord," she told him, "I believe that you are the Christ,[b] the Son of God, who was to come into the world."

### Jesus Raises Lazarus From the Dead

³⁸Jesus, once more deeply moved, came to the tomb. It was a cave with a stone laid across the entrance. ³⁹"Take away the stone," he said.

"But, Lord," said Martha, the sister of the dead man, "by this time there is a bad odor, for he has been there four days."

⁴⁰Then Jesus said, "Did I not tell you that if you believed, you would see the glory of God?"

⁴¹So they took away the stone. Then Jesus looked up and said, "Father, I thank you that you have heard me. ⁴²I knew that you always hear me, but I said this for the benefit of the people standing here, that they may believe that you sent me."

⁴³When he had said this, Jesus called in a loud voice, "Lazarus, come out!" ⁴⁴The dead man came out, his hands and feet wrapped with strips of linen, and a cloth around his face.

Jesus said to them, "Take off the grave clothes and let him go."

⁴⁵Therefore many of the Jews who had come to visit Mary, and had seen what Jesus did, put their faith in him. ⁴⁶But some of them went to the Pharisees and told them what Jesus had done. ⁴⁷Then the chief priests and the Pharisees called a meeting of the Sanhedrin.

[a]18 Greek *fifteen stadia* (about 3 kilometers)  [b]27 Or *Messiah*

# Group Questions

## TO BEGIN / 15 Minutes (Choose 1 or 2)

❏ When were you called to the death-bed of a close friend or relative whom you loved very much?

❏ What is the saddest funeral you remember attending?

❏ How are you at comforting people when they are going through grief?

## READ SCRIPTURE AND DISCUSS / 30 Minutes

❏ What was Jesus' relationship with Lazarus' family?

❏ How long had Lazarus been dead when Jesus arrived? How would you feel if you were Martha and Mary and you heard that Jesus had finally come?

❏ What do you learn about Martha from the way she talks to Jesus in verses 21–27? How does Jesus stretch her faith by his claim in verses 25–26?

❏ If Martha had faith (v. 22) in Jesus, why was she skeptical when Jesus asked them to remove the stone (v. 39)?

❏ Some Bible scholars question this miracle. What did those who were present at the tomb think about it? What happened when the Pharisees heard about it?

❏ What is the closest you have come to seeing a miracle like the one described here?

❏ If you had to compare your spiritual life to Lazarus in this story, where would you be: Still in the grave? Alive but still wrapped with grave clothes? Alive and free of the grave clothes?

## TO CLOSE AND PRAY / 15–30 Minutes

❏ As you look back over the time you have been in this group, what has happened in your spiritual life?

❏ How has this group helped to unwrap the grave clothes of your past and set you free?

❏ What still holds you in bondage that this group can pray about?

# Notes

**Summary.** It is one thing for Jesus to walk on water; it is another for him to overcome death. On one level this is another nature miracle: Jesus undoes the law of nature that all things die and once dead, cannot be brought back to life. But on another level, this is a whole new category of miracle. To bring life out of death is to do the work of creation. Truly only God can do such a thing. The raising of Lazarus is the ultimate demonstration of Jesus' miracle working power.

Lazarus is not the first or the only person Jesus raised from the dead. In Mark 5:21–24, 35–43 Jesus raises Jairus' daughter from the dead. And in Luke 7:11–17 he raises the widow's son from the dead. Jairus' daughter had just died when Jesus came and the widow's son was on the way to being buried (bodies were buried as soon after death as could be arranged; see Acts 5:5–6). So it might be claimed that they were not really dead but only in a coma. However, in this case the point is made that Lazarus is truly dead, so much so that his body has begun to decompose. There can be no doubt that Jesus raised a dead man back to life.

In the Gospel of John this is the last of the seven signs of Jesus' glory which John records (2:1–11; 4:46–54; 5:1–11; 6:1–13, 16–20; 9:1–7). It serves both to enact the truth Jesus taught concerning his power to give life (5:28–30) and to foreshadow his own death and resurrection.

**11:1 *He was from Bethany.*** Lazarus is identified in terms of where he lived and who his sisters were. Thus he is distinguished from other men in the NT by the same name such as Lazarus the beggar in Luke 16:20.

***Mary and her sister Martha.*** John's readers would have been familiar with these two sisters. Luke tells the story of an earlier visit on the part of Jesus in which Mary is identified as a disciple of Jesus while Martha is gently chided for being too preoccupied with her work (Luke 10:38–42). Here in this story, however, Martha becomes a disciple of Jesus. She is one of the first people to understand who he really is and to declare her faith in him (John 11:25–27).

**11:2** John refers to Mary in terms of an incident that his readers knew about even though John does not himself tell that story until chapter 12:3–8. In Mark's account of the story of the anointing, Jesus states: "I tell you the truth, wherever the gospel is preached throughout the world, what she has done will also be told, in memory of her" (Mark 14:9). And, indeed, even here Mary is referred to by this act.

**11:3** Given Jesus' reputation as a healer it is not surprising that the sisters would send for him when their brother fell ill.

**the one you love.** Jesus and Lazarus were friends. Not only do the sisters remark on the love Jesus had for Lazarus but so do the villagers when they see that Jesus is moved to tears at the tomb of Lazarus (John 11:33–36). The only other person who is identified as "one whom Jesus loved" is the writer of the Gospel (John 13:23–25; 21:20–24).

**11:17 four days.** By the time Jesus reaches Bethany Lazarus is well and truly dead, so that the body has begun to decompose in the hot middle-eastern climate (see v. 39).

**11:19 many Jews.** The author accents the size of the crowds to show that this final public sign was seen by many. Furthermore, given the proximity of Bethany to Jerusalem, probably some of these were religious leaders. Later this event is reported to Sanhedrin (John 11:45–53).

**11:21 If you had been here, my brother would not have died.** Since Lazarus had died probably even before Jesus received the message, this is not a rebuke but an expression of regret. It implies faith that if Jesus had been on the scene before his death, Lazarus could have been saved.

**11:22 But I know.** Given her confusion in verse 39, when Jesus asks for the tomb to be opened, this is not an expectation that Jesus could do a miracle even now, but an expression of her belief that Jesus, had he been on the scene, could have healed Lazarus since "God gives you what you ask."

**11:23 will rise again.** The Pharisees and other Jewish groups believed in a general resurrection at the end of history. She would have understood Jesus' comment as simply an appropriate expression of comfort at a funeral.

**11:25 I am the resurrection and the life.** This claim would jar anyone at a funeral! By it Jesus focuses Martha's attention, not on the doctrine of the general resurrection, but on him as the source of that resurrection. This is a personalized way of expressing the truth he taught in more abstract terms in John 5:24–29, that "whoever hears my word and believes him who sent me has eternal life."

**will live, even though he dies.** Spiritual life that will not end at physical death is in view here. In this verse and in verse 26, Jesus is asserting his sovereign power over death and his ability to "give life to whom he is pleased to give it" (John 5:21). Given this framework, the actual resurrection of Lazarus will be a dramatic sign of the validity of his claim.

**11:26 Do you believe this?** Jesus directly confronts Martha with this claim. Does she see him only as a healer or as the Lord of life?

**11:27** In this verse Martha declares by means of four terms exactly who Jesus is. If one understands Jesus to be who Martha identifies him as, then it is no mystery that he can and does perform miracles, even the miracle of raising a dead man to life. This is one of several confessional statements in the Gospel of John (John 6:69; 16:30; 20:28). This is, in fact, the purpose of the Gospel: "These are written that you may believe that Jesus is the Christ, the Son of God, and that by believing you may have life in his name" (John 20:31).

**Lord.** This term can mean simply "Sir," a polite form of address. It probably means this is verse 21 when Martha refers to Jesus by it. But here, it is a declaration of who he is: not a Lord but the Lord, the Lord of Lords. After his resurrection he would be called "the Lord," a title which carried this weight.

**Christ.** This is the Greek term for Messiah. Martha acknowledges Jesus to be the promised One of God who has come to save his people and be their King (the Son of David).

**the Son of God.** But he was not just the Messiah of popular expectation—a King who would free his people—he was God's own son. He was divine. The meaning behind this title is that Jesus was "just like God," sharing God's essential nature just as a child shared the characteristics of its parents. But Jesus is not just a son of God (as all men and women are since they were created by God) but the Son of God—unique, the manifestation of God in human form.

# Notes (Continued)

*who was to come into the world.* Finally, she refers to the expectation that one day a leader like Moses or David would arise (Deut. 18:18). Jesus is that "one who invades that world and transforms it," again acknowledging his authority and divine commission (Michaels).

**11:38** *the tomb.* Tombs for people of importance were either vertical shafts or horizontal hollows, both covered by a stone. Since this tomb is carved out of a cave, it would probably be the former type.

**11:39** *bad odor.* Even if Martha knew of the others Jesus had raised, they were people who had been dead for only a short time. By the fourth day the actual decomposition of the body had begun and therefore no resuscitation could be possible.

**11:40** *Did I not tell you.* This may be a reference to the message in verse 4, where Jesus says: "The sickness will not end in death." Or he may be referring to his statement in verse 25 that one who believes in him will live even though he dies. The irony is that it is this final sign, which demonstrates his glory far more than any of the other signs, that finally leads the religious authorities to take specific steps to put him to death (11:53).

*the glory of God.* There is a double meaning here. The act of raising Lazarus from the dead would obviously be a divine act of power for only God can give life, yet the signs have consistently been regarded as demonstrations of Jesus' identity. They reveal his glory (John 2:11) and, based on them, people make decisions about who he is (John 6:14; 9:33). This final sign will reveal what has been alluded to all along—Jesus is divine. He shares the power and nature of the Father. What the prologue described in abstract terms (John 1:1–3) is clearly shown here.

**11:41** *looked up.* This was a common posture for prayer.

**11:42** *that they may believe that you sent me.* Lazarus' resurrection was to be a powerful sign of the Father's stamp of approval upon Jesus.

**11:44** *The dead man came out.* This is a foretaste of the experience all people will share at the final resurrection when "all who are in their graves will hear (Jesus') voice and come out" (John 5:28–29).

*wrapped with strips of linen.* While burial customs included wrapping the body with cloth and spices (Jn 19:40), this was not intended to preserve the body like the ancient Egyptian process of mummification.

*grave clothes.* Lazarus' resuscitation differs from Jesus' resurrection in that his grave clothes were still with him. He would still need them at some later time. In contrast, Jesus' grave clothes were left behind in the tomb, never to be needed again (John 20:6–8). Lazarus' coming to life only robbed death for a time: Jesus' resurrection spells the ultimate defeat of death's power.

# UNIT 12—Resurrection of Jesus / Luke 24:1–12

## Scripture

The Resurrection of Jesus

**24** On the first day of the week, very early in the morning, the women took the spices they had prepared and went to the tomb. ²They found the stone rolled away from the tomb, ³but when they entered, they did not find the body of the Lord Jesus. ⁴While they were wondering about this, suddenly two men in clothes that gleamed like lightning stood beside them. ⁵In their fright the women bowed down with their faces to the ground, but the men said to them, "Why do you look for the living among the dead? ⁶He is not here; he has risen! Remember how he told you, while he was still with you in Galilee:

⁷'The Son of Man must be delivered into the hands of sinful men, be crucified and on the third day be raised again.' " ⁸Then they remembered his words.

⁹When they came back from the tomb, they told all these things to the Eleven and to all the others. ¹⁰It was Mary Magdalene, Joanna, Mary the mother of James, and the others with them who told this to the apostles. ¹¹But they did not believe the women, because their words seemed to them like nonsense. ¹²Peter, however, got up and ran to the tomb. Bending over, he saw the strips of linen lying by themselves, and he went away, wondering to himself what had happened.

# Group Questions

**TO BEGIN / 15 Minutes** (Choose 1 or 2)

- ❑ What time do you usually get up in the morning?
- ❑ How do you feel about visiting the grave of someone you loved very much?
- ❑ When you were a child, how did you celebrate Easter?

## READ SCRIPTURE AND DISCUSS / 30 MINUTES

- ❑ Why do you think the women went to the tomb early in the morning? What must have been going through their minds as they approached the tomb?
- ❑ When they found the tomb empty, what would be their first thought? What did the angels do to comfort them?
- ❑ How did the disciples receive the news when the women told them about the empty tomb?
- ❑ Why would Peter want to go see for himself? What must have been going through his mind as he reached the tomb?
- ❑ How is this story of the resurrection of Christ similar to and different from the story of Lazarus in the last session?
- ❑ When did you come to understand the full meaning of the resurrection of Jesus Christ? Do you accept the resurrection of Jesus Christ from the dead as a mystery you do not understand ... or as a historical fact that you do understand?

## TO CLOSE AND PRAY / 15–30 Minutes

- ❑ As you look back upon this course, were your expectations fulfilled?
- ❑ How would you like to celebrate this course with your group next week?
- ❑ What would you like to do after this course is over?

**Summary.** Jesus died and then rose again from the dead. This is the pivotal miracle around which the Gospel rotates. Because Jesus rose from the dead he can offer to the whole human race—past, present, and future—forgiveness of sins and eternal life.

We have already seen Jesus' power over death with his friend Lazarus. But now he himself has to face that same power: "the last enemy," as St. Paul put it (1 Cor. 15:26). That Jesus actually died is insisted upon by all the Gospel writers. He did now go into some sort of trance-like state that made him appear to be dead. Nor did he have a near-death experience. He was fully and finally dead. He was "crucified, dead, and buried" is how the Apostle's Creed hammers home this point.

Jesus knew death was coming. He warned his disciples repeatedly that he would die (e.g., Mark 8:31; 9:32; 10:33–34). But they did not seem to hear him because what he was saying was so beyond their imaginations. They knew that Jesus was the long-promised Messiah (Mark 8:29). But they also knew—from their Jewish heritage—that Messiahs don't die. Messiahs win. Messiahs kill others—the enemies of God. Messiahs reign in Jerusalem. To imagine that the Messiah could die was too big a conceptual leap for them.

Nor did they hear Jesus when he added to his prediction that he would die the promise that he would rise again. This was even more unimaginable. For example, when Peter, James, and John were coming down from the Mount of Transfiguration Jesus ordered them not to tell anyone what they had seen until "the Son of Man had risen from the dead." This puzzles the disciples. They discuss together "what 'rising from the dead' meant" (Mark 9:9–10). The disciples just didn't get it. They couldn't get it, it seems, until the actual events themselves—Jesus' death and resurrection—would convince them.

The Gospel of Luke closes with the triumphant news of the resurrection and ascension of Jesus. Luke begins chapter 24 with the announcement of the resurrection by the angels to the women. Then he recounts two post-resurrection appearances. Luke ends the chapter (and his Gospel) with Jesus' ascension into heaven. He does not discuss any of the events in the 40-day interval between the resurrection and ascension. Luke's special emphasis is on how the death and resurrection of Jesus is the fulfillment of Jesus' prophecies (vv. 6–7) as well as the culmination of the OT witness to the Messiah (vv. 27, 45). It is this witness that gives meaning and purpose to his death and resurrection.

# Notes (Continued)

**24:1** On the first day of the week … This was early Sunday morning. The women who were at the crucifixion had followed Joseph and saw clearly where Jesus was entombed (Luke 23:55). Thus they would know where to go when they returned to attend to the body.

*spices.* Aromatic oils to anoint the body, not so much to preserve it as to honor it (much like people today would put flowers on a grave). Clearly they did not expect Jesus to have risen from the dead since the perfumes they bought would have been quite expensive.

**24:2** The stone was rolled away not so that the resurrected Jesus could leave the tomb but so that his disciples could see that it was empty (see John 20:8).

*the stone.* It would have been fairly easy to roll the huge, disc shaped stone down the groove cut for it so that it covered the opening, but once in place it would have been very difficult to push it back up the incline.

*tomb.* Typically such tombs had a large antechamber, with a small two foot high doorway at the back which led into the 6- or 7- foot burial chamber proper.

**24:3** *they did not find the body.* All accounts of the resurrection stress this point. The body of Jesus was gone.

**24:4** *two men.* Matthew 28:2–3 says they were angels: The description of their clothing here confirms that this is Luke's meaning too. As angels announced the birth of Jesus (1:26ff; 2:9ff), so they now announce his resurrection. Later, they will explain the meaning of the ascension (Acts 1:10).

**24:6** *He has risen!* Literally, the phrase is "He has been raised" showing that God is the one who accomplished this great act.

*Remember how he told you.* Jesus had predicted his death and resurrection (e.g. Luke 9:22). What made no sense at all at the time now begins to be full of meaning! The resurrection unlocked the teachings of Jesus which had so confused the disciples earlier (see also Luke 24;27,45).

**24:9** *the Eleven.* Judas had committed suicide (Matt. 27:5).

**24:10** *Mary Magdalene, Joanna.* All the Gospel writers include Mary as one of the witnesses of Jesus' resurrection. Under Jewish law, women were not considered reliable witnesses. However, Jesus had given new status to women in his ministry and now they become the first heralds of the message that he has risen.

*Mary the mother of James.* Literally, "Mary of James." Typically one would understand that to mean James' wife, but Mark 15:40 refers specifically to Mary as the mother of James. John 19:25 calls her the wife of Clopas.

**24:11–12** The disciples did not believe the women, but Peter was moved to visit the tomb and investigate. Seeing the grave clothes without the body did not yet produce faith in him; instead he was merely confused about what could have happened.

**24:12** *he saw the strips of linen lying by themselves.* John reports this curious fact in even greater detail (John 20:1–9). It was the custom to bind a dead body with strips of linen cloth. The head was bound with a separate cloth, leaving the face and neck bare. Sprinkled into the folds of cloth were a large amount of spices. (Nicodemus provided some 75 pounds of myrrh and aloes for this purpose [John 19:38–40]). Thus when Jesus rose from the dead he would have passed through the cloth (as he later did through doors) and the whole mass would have collapsed, with the head piece tumbling to the side alone. This is, in fact, what Peter saw. In John's fuller description, note is made of the fact that the headpiece was folded up by itself, separate from the linen" (John 20:7). The Greek word translated "folded up" means, in fact, "twirled," describing the rounded shape of the now empty head turban. Had the body been stolen the graves clothes would have been taken or, at least, unwound and tossed aside.

## Historical Facts and the Resurrection

Dead men stay dead. The whole weight of our human experience tells us that this is so. Death is the final curtain, the end of life. We don't challenge this fact. We know it to be true. For this reason, the resurrection of Jesus poses a substantial barrier to faith for some people.

Make no mistake. The resurrection is not some peripheral doctrine, that can be cast aside because it is an affront to reason. It is central to the gospel: "If Christ has not been raised, our preaching is useless and so is your faith" (1 Cor 15:14). So much hinges on the resurrection. For example:

- Jesus' veracity: He predicted that he would die and be raised again. If he was wrong in this matter, how can we trust what he tells us about matters such as the forgiveness of sins and life after death?

- Jesus' claims: He claimed to be the Son of God. The resurrection is one demonstration that this is so. If he is still dead, Jesus is merely another great religious leader.

- Jesus' promise of new life: He said "I am the resurrection and the life. He who believes in me will live, even though he dies" (John 11:25).

- Jesus' relationship with us: If Jesus is still dead, we cannot know him other than as a memory.

Thus, it is important to look at the data that supports the assertion that Jesus rose from the dead. While one cannot ever "prove" the resurrection—it is a unique event happening only once in history and thus outside the realm where empirical proof is possible—it can be shown that the weight of the evidence points to it having happened. And as Edward John Carnell asserted, faith "is a resting of the mind in the sufficiency of the evidences." The church has claimed that there is sufficient evidence to believe in the resurrection of Jesus:

- The Tomb Was Empty: Everyone agrees on this fact. Were it not so, first-century officials would have produced the body to quell the troubling preaching of the apostles that Jesus had risen from the dead.

- The Grave Clothes Were Undisturbed: The only way for the grave clothes to lie undisturbed as they did, was for Jesus to have risen through them (as he later did through doors).

- Jesus Appeared After His Resurrection: At least 12 separate appearances are described in the NT, including an appearance to some 500 people in Galilee (which Paul reports in 1 Cor 15:6). Had this not happened Paul would never have asserted it in this public letter with the implicit challenge to check it out since "most of [them] are still living."

- The Disciples Were Transformed: When Jesus was taken away, the disciples fled and went into hiding. Yet after the resurrection they appear in Jerusalem, openly preaching that Jesus has risen, despite being forbidden to do so by the very people who crucified Jesus. Only an encounter with the risen Lord could have caused this kind of inner transformation.

- The Church Was Founded: The fact that there are churches around the world today can be traced directly to the resurrection. This was at the heart of the apostles' message. Nothing else apart from the resurrection of Jesus can account for the existence of the church.

Christians need to study carefully the evidence for the miracle of the resurrection. The following books will help in this matter:

- *Basic Christianity* by John Stott (Eerdmans) 1957.

- *Who Moved the Stone* by Frank Morrison (Zondervan) 1987.

- *The Day Death Died: Did Jesus Christ Really Rise from the Dead?* by Michael Green (InterVarsity Press), 1982.

- *I Believe in the Resurrection of Jesus* by George Eldon Ladd (Eerdmans) 1975.

- *Evidence That Demands a Verdict* by Josh McDowell (Here's Life) 1990.

# UNIT 13—The Catch of Fish / John 21:1–14

## Scripture

Jesus and the Miraculous Catch of Fish

**21** *Afterward Jesus appeared again to his disciples, by the Sea of Tiberias. It hap-pened this way: ²Simon Peter, Thomas (called Didymus), Nathanael from Cana in Galilee, the sons of Zebedee, and two other disciples were together. ³"I'm going out to fish," Simon Peter told them, and they said, "We'll go with you." So they went out and got into the boat, but that night they caught nothing.*

*⁴Early in the morning, Jesus stood on the shore, but the disciples did not realize that it was Jesus.*

*⁵He called out to them, "Friends, haven't you any fish?"*

*"No," they answered.*

*⁶He said, "Throw your net on the right side of the boat and you will find some." When they did, they were unable to haul the net in because of the large number of fish.*

*⁷Then the disciple whom Jesus loved said to Peter, "It is the Lord!" As soon as Simon Peter heard him say, "It is the Lord," he wrapped his outer garment around him (for he had taken it off) and jumped into the water. ⁸The other disciples followed in the boat, towing the net full of fish, for they were not far from shore, about a hundred yards. ⁹When they landed, they saw a fire of burning coals there with fish on it, and some bread.*

*¹⁰Jesus said to them, "Bring some of the fish you have just caught."*

*¹¹Simon Peter climbed aboard and dragged the net ashore. It was full of large fish, 153, but even with so many the net was not torn. ¹²Jesus said to them, "Come and have breakfast." None of the disciples dared ask him, "Who are you?" They knew it was the Lord. ¹³Jesus came, took the bread and gave it to them, and did the same with the fish. ¹⁴This was now the third time Jesus appeared to his disciples after he was raised from the dead.*

# Group Questions

**TO BEGIN / 15 Minutes** (Choose 1 or 2)

❑ Where is the best fishing spot in your state?
❑ What is the biggest fish you have caught?
❑ How would you like fish for breakfast?

**READ SCRIPTURE AND DISCUSS / 30 Minutes**

❑ Where are these seven disciples now? Why do you think they went back there?
❑ In fishing all night using nets, do you think Peter was just on vacation, or is he giving up on his spiritual calling and returning to his old business?
❑ When Jesus appears on the shore and tells Peter to try fishing on the other side of the boat, what do you think that triggered in Peter's mind?
❑ In the Middle East, to eat a meal with someone who has wronged you is to forgive that person. Why do you think Jesus made breakfast for his disciples?
❑ What is special about this miracle?
❑ When Jesus called you to follow him, what were you doing? How often do you find yourself going back to those days?
❑ As you have studied the miracles of Jesus Christ in this course, what has this done to your spiritual faith?

**TO CLOSE AND PRAY / 15–30 Minutes**

❑ What has been the high point in this course for you?
❑ What has this group come to mean to you in this course?
❑ What miracle would you like them to pray for in your life?

# Notes

**Summary.** Jesus rose from the dead. He then appeared to disciples—alive, recognizable, and full of power. He was no ghost. He had a body. He ate with others. But it was a different kind of body. He came through locked doors (John 20:19). He walked with his followers and yet they did not at first recognize him (Luke 24:13–32). His was a resurrection body. In this account, the resurrected Jesus meets once again with his disciples.

There are two miracles in this account: The huge catch of fish and the appearance of Jesus who had been crucified. The first miracle is what we have come to expect from Jesus: He has power over nature. For him to bring about a spectacular catch of fish is in line with his other miracles (and he had done this once before, see Luke 5:1–11). The second miracle is the extraordinary one. For him to rise from the dead and appear to his disciples is one of the greatest of all miracles.

Some scholars feel that chapter 21 functions like an appendix to the Gospel of John, focusing on the disciples and thus forming a bridge from the life of Jesus into the ministry of the church. And certainly, John 20:30–31 sounds like a concluding statement. However, chapter 21 is clearly connected with what precedes it. It begins with the phrase "afterward Jesus appeared again to his disciples" and in verse 14 we learn that this is the third post-resurrection appearance by Jesus to his disciples, thus linking this chapter to the two previous appearances (John 20:19–23; 26–29). There is the same startled and joyous acclamation one finds at other appearances. Peter declares in John 21:7 "It is the Lord" just as Mary exclaimed "I have seen the Lord!" (John 20:18) and Thomas professes "My Lord and My God" (John 20:28).

**21:1 *Afterward.*** Literally, this is "after these things …" We do not know how long after the resurrection this incident took place. However, the disciples have had time to journey from Jerusalem back to Galilee.

***Sea of Tiberias.*** Tiberias was a city founded on the shore of the Sea of Galilee in AD 20 by Herod. By the time this Gospel was written, this new name for the Sea of Galilee had become well-known. At the close of Mark's Gospel (Mark 16:7) the angel tells the women that Jesus is going ahead of his disciples into Galilee and they are to follow him there.

**21:2** On this occasion seven of the disciples are together. Five are identified. The Sons of Zebedee are James and John (Mark 1:19–20). The two anonymous disciples may be unnamed since they have been not previously featured in the Gospel of John. Nathanael's name does not appear in any list of the Twelve (e.g., Mark 3:16–19). A common guess is that he is the Bartholomew whose name does appear.

**21:3 *I'm going out to fish.*** Peter, along with his brother Andrew and James and John were fishermen when Jesus called them (Mark 1:16–20). It is not surprising as they wait for the Lord in Galilee (as they have been instructed) that they should decide to go fishing. But, in fact, this action on their part has another, metaphoric, dimension to it. When Jesus called these four men to follow him he promised them: "I will make you fishers of men" (Mark 1:17). So far, this promise had not been fulfilled (nor could it be prior to Jesus' redeeming death and resurrection). On their own, the disciples are not going to become these sort of fishermen. They have labored all night and come up empty. But then Jesus comes and instructs them how to fish (v. 6), and they become successful. This is a vivid prediction of what is ahead for the disciples. They will be empowered by Jesus to become successful fishers of men.

***that night.*** Much of the fishing on the Sea of Galilee took place at night. Fishermen carried blazing torches that enabled them to spot schools of fish and sometimes drew fish to the surface. But this reference may also have a metaphoric sense. The disciples are still "in the dark" when it comes to what the risen Christ wants of them. At dawn they will see Jesus on shore and he will give them direction. In John 13:30 the same double meaning is found. Judas leaves the Last Supper in order to betray Jesus. John notes: "And it was night."

**21:4 *the disciples did not realize that it was Jesus.*** There are two other resurrection appearances in which Jesus is not immediately recognized (Luke 24:30; John 20:14). Paul speaks of the resurrected body as having a different type of splendor than the normal body (1 Cor. 15:40–42). Whether these men failed to recognize him because it was still early and therefore somewhat dark or if there was some type of transformation in Jesus' appearance that caused them to be unable to immediately identify him is not told, but verse 12 indicates that the latter is likely.

**21:6 *they were unable to haul the net in because of the large number of fish.*** The lack of success after fishing all night, the call to throw in the net one more time, and the particular emphasis on the response of Peter are all very similar to the miracle recorded at the beginning of Jesus' ministry in Luke 5:1–11. The repetition of such a miracle would underscore the emphasis which Jesus made at that time that, with him, they would be very successful as "fishers of men." This particular miracle at this time would have special meaning to Peter whose threefold denial of Christ must have plagued him with doubts about his ability to be an apostle.

**21:7 *the disciple whom Jesus loved.*** This is thought to be John, the author of the Gospel.

***It is the Lord!*** As Jesus' voice opened Mary's eyes to recognize him (John 20:15), so here the enormous catch of fish revealed him to the beloved disciple. It is significant that in all the resurrection appearances Jesus is called by this divine title (John 20:18,25). Just as he had said in John 8:28, the glorification that would be his through his death and resurrection sealed the belief of his followers in his divine identity.

***he wrapped his outer garment around him.*** This refers to tucking up his fisherman's smock so he could swim to shore.

**21:9 *a fire of burning coals.*** It is significant that the same word used in John 18:18 to describe the fire around which Peter was standing when he betrayed Jesus is used here to describe the fire at which Jesus will draw Peter back into the company of his disciples (see John 21:15–17). These are the only two uses of this term in the NT.

**21:11 *153.*** Although there have been many attempts from earliest times on to find a symbolic meaning for this number, there is no agreement whatsoever about what it might be! It appears that this is instead an instance of the author simply reporting the facts about a phenomenal event.

**21:12 *None.*** dared ask him, "Who are you?" In light of the confession of the beloved disciple in verse 7, it is difficult to know what the author intends by this statement. It somewhat parallels the experience of the disciples in Matthew 28:17 where, in the context of another resurrection appearance, some of his followers were still unsure about him. On the other

# Notes (Continued)

hand, the author may mean that their certainty about who he was meant they no longer had to ask this question. This is the question that had been asked of Jesus in various ways throughout the Gospel of John (John 4:12; 7:12,26,40–41; 8:25; 9:35–36). In contrast to the confusion the disciples experienced previously (see 16:17–18), now, their understanding of his identity and mission is complete.

**breakfast.** The Jesus that they met was no disembodied spirit. He was flesh and blood. They could see him and hear him and eat with him. He has hands and feet that allow him to kindle a fire on the beach. Jesus has been resurrected bodily. He had conquered death.

**21:13** *Jesus came, took the bread and gave it to them.* In the Gospel of John there is no account of the Last Supper. However, the words used here are very similar to words used at the Last Supper (see Mark 14:22). Furthermore, the bread and the fish are reminiscent of the feeding of the 5,000 where there is a clear parallel to the Eucharist (see Unit 8 and the notes for Mark 6:41). It is via participation in this meal that the disciples come to recognize who Jesus is. A similar thing happens in Luke 24:30–31. The disciples on the road to Emmaus meet a mysterious stranger whom they discover—in the breaking of the bread—to be Jesus. Down through the ages the church continues to celebrate the Lord's Supper in remembrance of Jesus (1 Cor 11:23–24). So too the church continues to recognize the presence of Jesus in the breaking of the bread.

**21:14** *the third time.* This is the third resurrection account described in John's Gospel (see John 20:19–23 and 24–29). Altogether some 12 appearances are described or alluded to in the NT. Jesus appeared to Mary Magdalene (Mark 16:9; John 20:11–18), to the women (Matthew 28:9–10), to Cleopas and his companion (Luke 24:13–35), to Simon (Luke 24:34; 1 Corinthians 15:15), to all the disciples except Thomas (John 20:19–23), to all the disciples (John 20:24–29), to the seven disciples at the Sea of Galilee (John 21; 1–14), to the disciples on a mountain in Galilee (Matthew 28:16–20), to more than 500 (1 Corinthians 15:6), to James, the brother of Jesus (1 Corinthians 15:7), to the disciples on Olivet at the ascension (Acts 1:4–11) and to Paul on his way to Damascus (Acts 9:3–7; 22:6–10; 26:12–18; 1 Cointhians. 9:1; 15:8). The post-resurrection appearances are important for a number of reasons. For one thing, they are part of the proof of Jesus' resurrection (along with the fact of the empty tomb, the collapsed and empty grave clothes, etc.). Second, they show that Jesus had conquered death. He was not simply a disembodied spirit who appeared as a ghost-like figure, a hallucination, or a vision. He was real and had a body. Third, they describe how it was that the disciples learned of their mission. Fourth, it was the encounter with the living Jesus that changed the disciples from frightened men in hiding to bold witnesses who changed the world. Finally, the post-resurrection appearances show to all of us that Jesus is still alive and thus that we can enter into a personal relationship with him even today.

# ACKNOWLEDGEMENTS

It is not possible (nor desirable) to tackle as formidable a subject as the Miracles of Jesus without the aid of others. The standard exegetical tools have, of course, been used: The Arndt and Gingrich, *Greek-English Lexicon of the New Testament; The Interpreter's Dictionary of the Bible.* Colin Brown (ed.), *Dictionary of New Testament Theology,* Vol. 11, *Miracle,* Grand Rapids, MI: Zondervan, 1978. In addition, reference has been made to a series of fine commentaries: Albright, W.F. and Mann, C.S., *Matthew,* (The Anchor Bible), Garden City, NY: Doubleday, 1971. Bailey, Kenneth E., *Poet and Peasant: Through Peasant Eyes,* Grand Rapids, MI: Eerdmans, 1983, Barclay, William, *The Gospel of Luke* (The Daily Study Bible Series), Philadelphia: The Westminster Press, 1976 (second edition). Karl Barth, *Evangelical Theology: An Introduction.* Brown, Raymond, *The Gospel of John,* The Anchor Bible Series, Garden City, NY: Doubleday and Co., 1970. etc. D. S. Cairns, *The Faith That Rebels,* Richard Smith Inc., 1930. Cranfield, C.E.B., *St. Mark,* London: Cambridge, 1939. Ellis, E. Earle, *The Gospel of Luke* (The New Century Bible Commentary), Grand Rapids, MI: Eerdmans, 1981. France, R. T., *Matthew* (Tyndale New Testament Commentaries), Grand Rapids, MI: William B. Eerdmans, 1985. Fuller, Reginald, H., *Interpreting the Miracles,* Philadelphia, PA: Westminster Press, 1963. Geldenhuys, J. Norval, *Commentary on the Gospel of Luke* (The New London Commentary on the New Testament), London: Marshal, Morgan and Scott, 1950. Hendrickson, William, *The Gospel of John* (New Testament Commentary), Grand Rapids, MI: Baker Book House, 1953. Hendricksen, William, *The Gospel of Luke* (New Testament Commentary) Grand Rapids, MI: Baker Book House, 1978. Hill, David, *The Gospel of Matthew,* (The New Century Bible Commentary) Grand Rapids, MI: Eerdmans, 1981. Mann, C. S., *Mark,* The Anchor Bible Series, Garden City, NY: Doubleday and Co., 1986. Marshall, I. Howard, *Commentary on Luke* (The New International Greek Testament Commentary) Grand Rapids, MI: Eerdmans Publishing Co., 1978. Michaels, J. Ramsey, *John* (A Good News Commentary), San Francisco: Harper and Row, 1984. Mounce, Robert H., *Matthew* (A Good News Commentary) San Francisco, CA: Harper and Row, 1985. Gerd Thiessen, *The Miracle Stories of the Early Christian Tradition,* Edinburgh: T&T Clark, 1983.

## Copyright Endorsements

Grateful acknowledgement is made to the following publisher for permission to reprint copyright material.

Units 1 and 9
Lewis, C. S., *Miracles,* © 1947, used by permission of William Collins Publishers, London.